CYBER-RISK MANAGEMENT FRAMEWORKS FOR DIGITAL ECOSYSTEMS

BY

Kalpit Sharma

CYBER-RISK MANAGEMENT FRAMEWORKS FOR DIGITAL ECOSYSTEMS

BY

Kalpit Sharma

Abstract

The success of digital behemoths like Google, Microsoft, Walmart, and Netflix, is attributed to their ecosystem approach (Iansiti and Levien 2004; Walker 2021). Digital ecosystems tend to behave like platforms that connect producers and consumers efficiently (Parker et al. 2016). For example, in Uber, Kickstarter, Nintendo, and AirBnB's ecosystem, today's consumers can become producers in the future (Parker et al. 2016). These platforms tend to operate as two-sided markets (Eisenmann et al. 2015), which thrives on the principle of network effect (Hinz et al. 2020) (i.e., economic value = n^2, where n is the number of individuals enrolled on the platform) (Jiang et al. 2018). This thesis models the cyber-risk assessment, quantification, mitigation strategies for three multi-stakeholder digital ecosystems: online gaming platforms, smart cities, and crowdfunding platforms, using the concepts of data mining, machine learning, and econometrics methods.

In the first study, we observe that online gaming platforms like Steam, Twitch, PlayStation, and Xbox, host Massively Multiplayer Online Games (MMOG) (such as Final Fantasy, World of Warcraft (WoW), and PlayerUnknown's Battleground (PUBG)) developed by firms such as Blizzard, Nintendo (Yahyavi and Kemme 2013). These platforms are popular entertainment options for young individuals with a high disposable income; thus, frequent targets of Distributed-Denial-of-Service (DDoS) attacks by hackers, despite legal deterrence. In this context, using the Protection-Motivation theory (PMT) (Herath and Rao 2009; Rogers 1975) and Rational-Choice theory (RCT) (Becker 1990; Cavusoglu et al. 2008; McCarthy 2002), we propose a framework to (i) assess the cyber-risk management (CRA), (ii) quantify cyber-risk (CRQ), and (iii) mitigate the cyber-risk (CRM) arising due to DDOS attacks on MMOG platforms (Campbell et al. 2003; Chatterjee et al. 2015; Gordon et al. 2003; Ransbotham 2021). We propose three different frameworks based on cyber-risk assessment methods (i.e., probability of DDoS attack): (i) generalized linear models (CRAMOG), (ii) Kernel naïve Bayes classifier (KB-CRAM), and (iii) feedforward neural networks (FNN-CRAM). We have analyzed the DDoS attack data specifically on MMOG forms as provided by CDN such as Akamai (McKeay 2017). We also incorporate the publically announced DDoS-specific vulnerability data from National Vulnerability Database (NVD) (NIST 2018). Next, we compute the expected loss to quantify the impact of a DDoS attack for MMOG platforms. Subsequently, we plot a 2×2 risk-severity heat matrix to aid the Chief Technology Officer (CTO) by suggesting ways to accept, reduce, or pass cyber-risk resulting from DDoS attacks using technology (i.e., cybersecurity tools, predictive algorithms) and cyber-insurance methods (Johansmeyer 2021; Kleindorfer and Kunreuther 1999; Kunreuther 1997).

After a DDoS attack is experienced, we also observe that third-party security experts analyze (i.e., sources, vulnerabilities, mitigation strategies) and post about them on public forums (such as zdnet.com). These forums help legal authorities and CTOs gather information about DDoS attacks and prepare their mitigation strategies accordingly. In this context, we propose a TCRAM framework to (i) assess the cyber-risk management, (ii) quantify cyber-risk, and (iii) mitigate the cyber-risk arising due to misinterpretation of critical themes related to DDOS attacks from web articles. Firstly, the CRA module analyzes textual web articles related to DDoS attacks from cybersecurity news outlets. Next, using Latent Dirichlet Allocation (Blei et al. 2003), we extract the critical themes. Subsequently, we estimate the probability of misinterpreting these themes using the Kernel naïve Bayes classifier. Next, the CRQ module calculates the expected loss incurred by a firm due to DDoS attacks. Lastly, the CRM module aids the CTO in reducing, accepting, or passing the cyber-risk using a mix of technological (i.e., cybersecurity tools, predictive algorithms) and cyber-insurance interventions.

In the third study, we have evaluated two scenarios related to smart city digital platforms. In this context, we model the smart city Integrated Traffic Management System (ITMS), which hackers attack by tampering with either electronic speed limit signs or ITMS speed sensors, disrupting the traffic services for the citizens (Kim et al. 2021). For example, an autonomous vehicle may misread a tampered electronic speed limit of 30 mph as 80 mph in the first scenario, resulting in an overspeeding-related collision. Similarly, 90 mph can be misread as 30 mph, resulting in congestion and subsequent loss of productive hours (Povolny and Trivedi 2020). As a result, it is estimated that 3% of the GDP is lost in most countries due to congestion and accidents resulting from traffic malfunctioning on city pathways (WHO 2018). Further, it may also lead to data loss, financial loss, and reputational damage to life-threatening disruption to essential city services like healthcare provision, transportation, law enforcement, power and utilities, and residential services. In this context, using the PMT (Herath and Rao 2009; Rogers 1975) and RCT (Becker 1990; Cavusoglu et al. 2008; McCarthy 2002), we propose a DL-CRAM framework to (i) assess the cyber-risk management, (ii) quantify cyber-risk, and (iii) mitigate the cyber-risk arising due to hacker-induced tampering of electronic speed limit signs (Povolny and Trivedi 2020; Schneider 2018). Our CRA module uses a Convolutional Neural Network (CNN) algorithm (LeCun et al. 1989), takes publically available images of electronic two-digit speed limit sign as an input, learns its features, and outputs the probability of misreading. Then, using the Bayesian inference model, we compute the conditional probability of an autonomous vehicle misreading both the digits or one of the two digits. Subsequently, based on the concepts of risk theory, the CRQ module calculates the expected loss for a smart city due to collision or congestion on the pathways. In line with the coping appraisal component of PMT, our CRM module proposes strategies for the smart-city administrator to reduce cyber-risk using technological means (i.e., cybersecurity tools, predictive algorithms) and pass the residual risk to third-party cyber-insurer.

In the second scenario related to the smart city digital ecosystem, we assume that hacker has compromised ITMS speed sensors resulting in collision and congestion. For example, on a particular street, vehicles were traveling at an average speed of 30 kmph. However, hackers can compromise the ITMS sensors, such that a driver reads it as 80 kmph. It will lead to congestion by routing the traffic through other pathways and subsequent loss of productive hours (Povolny and Trivedi 2020). In this context, using the PMT (Herath and Rao 2009; Rogers 1975), we propose a Seasonal ARIMA (SARIMA) based Cyber-risk Assessment, and Mitigation framework for smart cities (SCRAM) to (i) assess the cyber-risk management, (ii) quantify cyber-risk, and (iii) mitigate the cyber-risk arising due to hacker-induced tampering of ITMS speed sensors (Povolny and Trivedi 2020; Schneider 2018). Our CRA module uses a Seasonal time series (i.e., SARIMA) forecasting method (Box 2016), takes publically available ITMS average speed data from the city of Aarhus as an input, and outputs the probability of anomalies in the average speed of vehicles. Subsequently, based on the concepts of risk theory, the cyber-risk quantification (CRQ) module calculates the expected loss for a smart city due to collision or congestion on the pathways. In line with the coping appraisal component of PMT, our CRM module proposes strategies for the smart-city administrator to reduce cyber-risk using technological means (i.e., cybersecurity tools, predictive algorithms)and pass the residual risk to third-party cyber-insurer.

The final study deals with the crowdfunding platforms where campaign creators and campaign backers interact with funding the potential campaign (such as Kickstarter, Milaap, Indiegogo) (Burtch et al. 2013; Gleasure and Morgan 2018). It is commonly observed that these platforms tend to have a substantial number of fraud campaigns hosted on them (Carpenter 2017; NBC 2014). In this context, we posit a blockchain-based framework for cyber-risk assessment and mitigation (BCRAM) for crowdfunding platforms (Liang et al. 2021; Sarker et al. 2021). Our framework takes platform data from Kickstarter with the campaign and creator-specific traits. Thereafter, using the Kernel naïve Bayes classifier, we predict the probability of correctly classifying the success of the campaigns. Next, we calculate the loss of platform fees associated with misclassified campaigns. Subsequently, this framework suggests ways to reduce the instances of fraud campaigns using a consortium-based blockchain solution for data integrity issues for the platform. Any subsequent losses may be passed onto cyber-insurer (AIRS 2019; Burtch et al. 2013; Mollick and Nanda 2016; Xu et al. 2021).

Table of Contents

List of Figures.. xiii
List of Tables xviii
List of Abbreviations xxi
Acknowledgments xxiv

1. **Introduction** 3
   1.1. Digital Ecosystems... 3
       1.1.1. Massively Multiplayer Online Gaming (MMOG) platforms 5
       1.1.2. Smart cities... 11
       1.1.3. Crowdfunding platforms 13
   1.2. Cyber-risk Management... 16
   1.3. Thesis contributions 17
       1.3.1. Academic contributions 17
       1.3.2. Managerial implications.. 19
   1.4. Organization of the thesis 20

2. **Literature Review** 23
   2.1. Cyber-risk Management... 23
       2.1.1. Cyber-risk Assessment (CRA) 24
       2.1.2. Cyber-risk Quantification (CRQ) 27
       2.1.3. Cyber-risk Mitigation (CRM) 34
   2.2. Digital Ecosystems... 36
       2.2.1. Massively Multiplayer Online Gaming (MMOG) platforms........ 36
       2.2.2. Smart cities... 38
       2.2.3. Crowdfunding platforms 40

3. **Research questions** 42
   3.1. Massively Multiplayer Online Gaming (MMOG) platforms............... 43
       3.1.1. Kernel naïve Bayes classifier-based cyber-risk assessment and mitigation framework for online gaming platforms (KB-CRAM)....................... 43
       3.1.2. A logit-based Cyber-risk Assessment and Mitigation model for Massively Multiplayer Online Gaming (CRAMOG) platforms 48

3.1.3. Cyber-risk management framework for online gaming firms: An Artificial Neural Network approach (FNN-CRAM) 53

3.1.4. Text mining-based cyber-risk assessment for DDoS attacks and mitigation using cyber-insurance (TCRAM) 61

3.2. Smart Cities 65

3.2.1. SARIMA-based cyber-risk assessment and mitigation model for a smart city's traffic management systems (SCRAM) 66

3.2.2. Cyber-risk Assessment and Mitigation framework for smart cities: A deep learning approach (DL-CRAM) 69

3.3. Crowdfunding platforms 73

3.3.1. Cyber-risk Assessment (CRA) 74

3.3.2. Cyber-risk Quantification (CRQ) 77

3.3.3. Cyber-risk Mitigation (CRM) 77

4. Methodology 79

4.1. Massively Multiplayer Online Gaming (MMOG) platforms 79

4.1.1. Kernel naïve Bayes classifier-based cyber-risk assessment and mitigation framework for online gaming platforms (KB-CRAM) 80

4.1.2. A logit-based Cyber-risk Assessment and Mitigation model for Massively Multiplayer Online Gaming (CRAMOG) platforms 83

4.1.3. Cyber-risk management framework for online gaming firms: An Artificial Neural Network approach (FNN-CRAM) 84

4.1.4. Text mining-based cyber-risk assessment for DDoS attacks and mitigation using cyber-insurance (TCRAM) 87

4.2. Smart Cities 90

4.2.1. SARIMA-based cyber-risk assessment and mitigation model for a smart city's traffic management systems (SCRAM) 91

4.2.2. Cyber-risk Assessment and Mitigation framework for smart cities: A deep learning approach (DL-CRAM) 94

4.3. Crowdfunding platforms 96

5. Data 98

5.1. Massively Multiplayer Online Gaming (MMOG) platforms 98

5.1.1. Kernel naïve Bayes classifier-based cyber-risk assessment and mitigation framework for online gaming platforms (KB-CRAM) 98

5.1.2. A logit-based Cyber-risk Assessment and Mitigation model for Massively Multiplayer Online Gaming (CRAMOG) platforms 100

5.1.3. Cyber-risk management framework for online gaming firms: An Artificial Neural Network approach (FNN-CRAM) 101

5.1.4. Text mining-based cyber-risk assessment for DDoS attacks and mitigation using cyber-insurance (TCRAM) 104

5.2. Smart Cities 109

5.2.1. SARIMA-based cyber-risk assessment and mitigation model for a smart city's traffic management systems (SCRAM) 110

5.2.2. Cyber-risk Assessment and Mitigation framework for smart cities: A deep learning approach (DL-CRAM) 112

5.3. Crowdfunding platforms 112

5.3.1. Creator-specific traits 119

5.3.2. Platform-specific traits 119

6. **Results** 121

6.1. Massively Multiplayer Online Gaming (MMOG) platforms 121

6.1.1. Kernel naïve Bayes classifier-based cyber-risk assessment and mitigation framework for online gaming platforms (KB-CRAM) 121

6.1.2. A logit-based Cyber-risk Assessment and Mitigation model for Massively Multiplayer Online Gaming (CRAMOG) platforms 128

6.1.3. Cyber-risk management framework for online gaming firms: An Artificial Neural Network approach (FNN-CRAM) 135

6.1.4. Text mining-based cyber-risk assessment for DDoS attacks and mitigation using cyber-insurance (TCRAM) 147

6.2. Smart Cities 161

6.2.1. SARIMA-based cyber-risk assessment and mitigation model for a smart city's traffic management systems (SCRAM) 162

6.2.2. Cyber-risk Assessment and Mitigation framework for smart cities: A deep learning approach (DL-CRAM) 176

6.3. Crowdfunding platforms 184

6.3.1. Cyber-risk Assessment (CRA) 184

6.3.2. Cyber-risk Quantification (CRQ) 184

6.3.3. Cyber-risk Mitigation (CRM) 186

7. **Discussion** 189

    7.1. Massively Multiplayer Online Gaming (MMOG) platforms............................ 189

        7.1.1. Kernel naïve Bayes classifier-based cyber-risk assessment and mitigation framework for online gaming platforms (KB-CRAM).. 189

        7.1.2. A logit-based Cyber-risk Assessment and Mitigation model for Massively Multiplayer Online Gaming (CRAMOG) platforms 192

        7.1.3. Cyber-risk management framework for online gaming firms: An Artificial Neural Network approach (FNN-CRAM) 195

        7.1.4. Text mining-based cyber-risk assessment for DDoS attacks and mitigation using cyber-insurance (TCRAM) 198

    7.2. Smart Cities.. 201

        7.2.1. SARIMA-based cyber-risk assessment and mitigation model for a smart city's traffic management systems (SCRAM).. 202

        7.2.2. Cyber-risk Assessment and Mitigation framework for smart cities: A deep learning approach (DL-CRAM)... 205

    7.3. Crowdfunding platforms 207

8. Conclusion 210
9. Appendix 213

    9.1. Blockchain 213

    9.2. Performance plots for training process on monthly data 217

    9.3. Probability estimates from FNN for monthly 219

List of Figures

Figure 1.1 Overview of Digital Ecosystems 4

Figure 1.2: Stakeholders of an MMOG firm 7

Figure 1.3(a): DDoS attacks on different industries (2018-2019) 10

Figure 1.3(b): Revenue loss due to the decrease in service level of MMOG offerings 10

Figure 1.4: Stakeholders of a Smart city 12

Figure 1.5: Stakeholder view of crowdfunding platforms 15

Figure 1.6: Broad overview of thesis in terms of methodologies used 21

Figure 2.1: Broad overview of the literature in this thesis 23

Figure 2.2: Overview of Cyber-risk Quantification (CRQ) methods 27

Figure 3.1: Overview of studies in terms of cyber-risk management modules 42

Figure 3.2: Overview of the process-view approach for MMOG-related studies 43

Figure 3.3 Proposed Model for KB-CRAM 44

Figure 3.4: Proposed model for CRAMOG framework 49

Figure 3.5: FNN-CRAM model for MMOG firms 54

Figure 3.6: Cyber-risk assessment module for FNN-CRAM model 55

Figure 3.7: Stakeholder view of DDoS attack lifecycle 57

Figure 3.8: Flowchart of the proposed TCRAM model 63

Figure 3.9: Overview of cyber-risk management frameworks related to smart cities 65

Figure 3.10: Proposed SCRAM model 68

Figure 3.11: Proposed DL-CRAM model 70

Figure 3.12: Proposed BCRAM model 74

Figure 3.13: Diagram for Cyber-risk Assessment module 75

Figure 4.1: Overview of methodologies used for MMOG platforms 79

Figure 4.2: Overview of studies related to smart cities 90

Figure 4.3: ACF plot of the average speed of vehicles in February (n=111) 91

Figure 5.1: Overview of studies related to MMOG platforms 98

Figure 5.2: Types of tokens in the text corpus 104

Figure 5.3: Frequency chart for most frequent words in the text corpus 105

Figure 5.4(a): Word cloud on negative sentiment words 107

Figure 5.4(b): Frequency chart on negative sentiment words 107

Figure 5.5(a): Word cloud on positive sentiment words 108

Figure 5.5(b): Frequency chart on positive sentiment words 108

Figure 5.6 Overview of studies related to smart cities 109

Figure 5.7: Dendrogram for the original dataset (n=452) 115

Figure 5.8(a): Clustering after removing outliers from the original dataset (n = 447) 116

Figure 5.8(b): Fitted exponential distribution for pledged amount 116

Figure 5.9(a): Campaign title length Vs. Amount pledged by backers 117

Figure 5.9(b): Number of projects V/s Project Duration (in weeks) 117

Figure 5.10(a): Count of all projects according to launch year 118

Figure 5.10(b): Count of all successful projects according to launch year 119

Figure 6.1: Overview of studies related to MMOG platforms 121

Figure 6.2(a) : Dendrogram for splitting Class E 123

Figure 6.2(b) : Dendrogram for splitting Class C 123

Figure 6.3: Risk Mitigation Heat Matrix (After the last iteration) 127

Figure 6.4: Residual analysis of predicted probability (M1) for each DDoS attack (Time: 2017 Q2 to 2018 Q2) 131

Figure 6.5: Risk-Severity heat matrix for MMOG firm 134

Figure 6.6(a): Performance plot of FNN for quarterly NTPFlood data 135

Figure 6.6(b): Performance plot of FNN for quarterly SSDPFlood data 136

Figure 6.6(c): Performance plot of FNN for quarterly UC data 136

Figure 6.6(d): Performance plot of FNN for quarterly UD data 137

Figure 6.6(e): Performance plot of FNN for quarterly UDPFlood data 137

Figure 6.7(a): Probability estimates from FNN for quarterly NTPFlood data 139

Figure 6.7(b): Probability estimates from FNN for quarterly SSDPFlood data 139

Figure 6.7(c): Probability estimates from FNN for quarterly UC data 140

Figure 6.7(d): Probability estimates from FNN for quarterly UD data 140

Figure 6.7(e): Probability estimates from FNN for quarterly UDPFlood data 141

Figure 6.8(a): Weibull distribution for NTP 143

Figure 6.8(b): Weibull distribution for SSDP 143

Figure 6.8(c): Weibull distribution for UC 143

Figure 6.8(d): Weibull distribution for UD 143

Figure 6.8(e): Weibull distribution for UDP Flood 143

Figure 6.9(a): E(L): Gamma distribution for NTP Flood 145

Figure 6.9(b): E(L): Gamma distribution for SSDP Flood 145

Figure 6.9(c): E(L): Gamma distribution for UC 146

Figure 6.9(d): E(L): Gamma distribution for UD 146

Figure 6.10: Risk-Severity heat matrix 146

Figure 6.11(a): Elbow curve for bigram model 148

Figure 6.11(b): Elbow curve for trigram model 148

Figure 6.12(a): Topic 1 151

Figure 6.12(b): Topic probability of keywords 151

Figure 6.13(a): Topic 3 152

Figure 6.13(b): Topic probability of keywords 152

Figure 6.14(a): Topic 5 153

Figure 6.14(b): Topic probability of keywords..153

Figure 6.15(a): Topic 2 154

Figure 6.15(b): Topic probability of keywords..155

Figure 6.16(a): Topic 7 155

Figure 6.16(b): Topic probability of keywords..156

Figure 6.17(a): Topic 6 157

Figure 6.17(b): Topic probability of keywords..157

Figure 6.18: ROC curve for trigram model 158

Figure 6.19: Gamma distribution for the expected loss 160

Figure 6.20: Risk-Severity heat matrix...160

Figure 6.21: Overview of studies related to smart cities 161

Figure 6.22(a): Actual and fitted values for February*..163

Figure 6.22(b): Anomalous average speeds for February...163

Figure 6.22(c): Actual and fitted values for March*..164

Figure 6.22(d): Anomalous average speeds for March...164

Figure 6.22(e): Actual and fitted values for April*..165

Figure 6.22(f): Anomalous average speeds for April 165

Figure 6.22(g): Actual and fitted values for May*...166

Figure 6.22(h): Anomalous average speeds for May...166

Figure 6.22(i): Actual and fitted values for June*...167

Figure 6.22(j): Anomalous average speeds for June...167

Figure 6.22(k): Actual and fitted values for August*..168

Figure 6.22(l): Anomalous average speeds for August 168

Figure 6.22(m): Actual and fitted values for September*...169

Figure 6.22(n): Anomalous average speeds for September..169

Figure 6.23(o): Actual and fitted values for October* 170

Figure 6.24 p): Anomalous average speeds for October 170

Figure 6.22(q): Actual and fitted values for November* 171

Figure 6.22(r): Anomalous average speeds for November* 171

Figure 6.23: Beta distribution curve for the probability of attacks on an ITMS sensor 173

Figure 6.24: Gamma distribution curve for expected loss values due to tampering of ITMS sensor 174

Figure 6.25: Risk Mitigation Heat matrix 175

Figure 6.26(a): Expected loss in NY scenario 181

Figure 6.26(b): Expected loss in NN scenario 181

Figure 6.27: Risk-Severity heat matrix (n_{NN} =6, n_{YN} = 447, n_{NY} = 447, n_{total} = 2910) 183

Figure 6.28: Risk-Severity Heat Matrix 187

Figure 9.1: Performance plot of FNN for monthly NTPFlood data 217

Figure 9.2: Performance plot of FNN for monthly SSDPFlood data 217

Figure 9.3: Performance plot of FNN for monthly UC data 218

Figure 9.4: Performance plot of FNN for monthly UD data 218

Figure 9.5: Performance plot of FNN for monthly UDPFlood data 219

Figure 9.6 Probability estimates from FNN for monthly NTPFlood data 219

Figure 9.7: Probability estimates from FNN for monthly SSDPFlood data 220

Figure 9.8: Probability estimates from FNN for monthly UC data 220

Figure 9.9: Probability estimates from FNN for monthly UD data 221

Figure 9.10: Probability estimates from FNN for monthly UDPFlood data 221

List of Tables

Table 1.1: Data description of popular MMOG/ MMORPGs 5
Table 1.2: DDoS variants and their characteristics 9
Table 1.3: Smart city attack incidents 13
Table 2.1 Cyber-risk Assessment methods 25
Table 2.2: Cyber-risk Quantification methods 30
Table 2.3: Text mining in Cybersecurity literature 32
Table 2.4: Cyber-risk mitigation through technological interventions 34
Table 2.5: Cyber-risk mitigation through financial interventions 36
Table 2.6: Cybersecurity issues in smart cities 39
Table 3.1: Relationship between DDoS attack class and DDoS attack types 45
Table 3.2: Model variables and relevant literature support 45
Table 3.3: Model variables and relevant literature support 55
Table 3.4: Relevant inputs and their literature support 62
Table 3.5: Relevant variables and their literature support 67
Table 3.6: Relevant variables and their literature support 71
Table 3.7: Impact of misreading speeds 72
Table 3.8: Relevant variables and their literature support 76
Table 4.1: Steps in the KB-CRAM model 82
Table 4.2: Steps in the FNN-CRAM model 86
Table 4.3: Pre-processing steps for the text from web articles 87
Table 4.4: Steps in the TCRAM model 90
Table 4.5: Stationarity and Seasonality test for an average speed of vehicles 92
Table 4.6: Steps in the DL-CRAM Model 95
Table 5.1: Summary statistics (2012 Q2 to 2018 Q2) 99
Table 5.2: Correlation matrix (N=10,329) 99
Table 5.3: Summary statistics (2012 Q2 to 2018 Q2) 100
Table 5.4: Correlation matrix (N = 95) 101
Table 5.5: Summary statistics for the attack dataset (from 2012 Q2 (t_1) to 2018 Q2 (t_{25})) ... 102

Table 5.6: Descriptive statistics of hourly average speed of vehicles (N_{total} = 5077) 110
Table 5.7: Description of training and testing for SARIMA model 111
Table 5.8: Dataset composition 112
Table 5.9: Descriptive Statistics of the reduced dataset (n=447) 113
Table 5.10: Correlation Matrix for variables (n=447) 114
Table 6.1: Probability of Correct Classification for Testing Dataset (n=4,132) 122
Table 6.2: Probability of Correct Classification for Testing Dataset (n=4,132) 124
Table 6.3: Performance Metric for each DDoS attack class[*] 125
Table 6.4: Risk-Expected Loss Matrix[#] 126
Table 6.5: Coefficients of logit and probit models 129
Table 6.6: Beta parameter estimates for risk distribution 132
Table 6.7: Gamma parameter estimates for expected loss distribution 133
Table 6.8: Mean-squared error (MSE) for each attack during training 138
Table 6.9: Probability of DDoS attacks for the testing window 141
Table 6.10: Weibull parameter estimates for risk distribution 142
Table 6.11: Expected Loss for the testing dataset 144
Table 6.12: Gamma parameter estimates for expected loss distribution 145
Table 6.13: Top 5 keywords in topic clusters 149
Table 6.14: Confusion Matrix for Testing Dataset 159
Table 6.15: SARIMA model parameters 162
Table 6.16: Probability of mispredicting the average speed from the testing dataset 172
Table 6.17: Expected Loss for each month 173
Table 6.18: Confusion matrix for the testing dataset using CNN model for digit recognition (n = 4,000) 176
Table 6.19: Speed limit misreading for NY scenario 177
Table 6.20: Impact of misreading speeds (YN scenario) (n = 27) 178
Table 6.21: Speed limit misreading for NN scenario 179
Table 6.22: Impact on smart-city due to misreading of speeds 182
Table 6.23: Confusion Matrix for ($n_{testing}$=136) 184
Table 6.24: Risk and Severity values for campaigns ($n_{testing}$ = 136) 185
Table 6.25: Risk-Impact values for misclassified campaigns 185

Table 9.1: Literature related to blockchain and its benefits...214
Table 9.2: Examples of blocks in a crowdfunding blockchain..216

List of Abbreviations

ACF	Autocorrelation Function
AIC	Akaike's Information Criteria
B2P	Box-to-Play
BCRAM	Blockchain-based Cyber-risk Assessment and Mitigation
BFSI	Banking, Financial Services and Insurance
BIC	Bayesian Information Criteria
bps	Bits per second
CAGR	Compunded Annual Growth Rate
CAIDA	Center for Applied Internet Data Analysis
CART	Classification and Regression Trees
CDN	Content Delivery Network
CERT	Community Emergency Response Team
CIA	Confidentiality-Integrity-Availability
CNN	Convolutional Neural Network
CRA	Cyber-risk Assessment
CRAMOG	Cyber-risk Assessment and Mitigation for Online Games
CRM	Cyber-risk Mitigation
CRQ	Cyber-risk Quantification
CTO	Chief Technology Officer
CVE	Common Vulnerabilities and Exposures
CVSS	Common Vulnerability Scoring System
DDoS	Distributed Denial-of-Service
DL-CRAM	Deep learning-based Cyber-risk Assessment and Mitigation
DNS	Domain Name Server
DoS	Denial-of-Service
F2P	Free-to-Play
FNN	Feedforward Neural Network
FNN-CRAM	Feedforward Neural Network-based Cyber-risk Assessment and Mitigation
FPS	First Person Shooter

GARCH	Generalized Autoregressive Conditional Heteroskedasticity	
GLM	Genralized Linear Models	
GSA	Gaming Standards Association	
ICMP	Internet Control Message Protocol	
ICO	Initial Coin Offering	
ISP	Internet Service Provider	
ITMS	Integrated Traffic Management System	
KNB	Kernel Naïve Bayes	
LDA	Latent Dirichlet Allocation	
MMOG	Massively Multiplayer Online Games	
MMORPG	Massively Multiplayer Online Role-Playing Games	
MNIST	Modified National Institute of Standards and Technology database	
MSE	Mean-Squared Error	
MSSP	Managed Security Service Provider	
NIST	National Institute of Standards and Technology	
NTP	Network Time Protocol	
NVD	National Vulnerability Database	
P2P	Pay-to-Play	
PCI-DSS	Payment Card Industry Data Security Standard	
PDF	Probability Density Function	
PMT	Protection-Motivation Theory	
pps	Packets per second	
RCT	Rational Choice Theory	
ROC	Receiver Operating Characteristics	
SARIMA	Seasonal Autoregressive Integrated Moving Average	
SCRAM	SARIMA-based Cyber-risk Assessment and Mitigation	
SSDP	Simple Service Discovery Protocol	
SVM	Support Vector Machine	
TCP	Transmission Control Protocol	
TCRAM	Text mining-based Cyber-risk Assessment and Mitigation	
tf-idf	Term Frequency–Inverse Document Frequency	
UC	UDP Fragment and CharGEN	

UD	UDP Fragment and DNS Flood	
UDP	User Datagram Protocol	
URL	Uniform Resource Locator	
VaR	Value-at-Risk	
VC	Venture Capitalist	
vC	Vulnerability count	
vscr	Vulnerability Score	

1. Introduction

1.1. Digital Ecosystems

The success of digital behemoths like Google, Microsoft, Walmart, and Netflix, is attributed to their ecosystem approach (Iansiti and Levien 2004; Walker 2021). Digital ecosystems tend to behave like platforms that connect producers and consumers efficiently (Parker et al. 2016). For example, in Uber, Kickstarter, Nintendo, and AirBnB's ecosystem, today's consumers can become producers in the future (Parker et al. 2016). These platforms tend to operate as two-sided markets (Eisenmann et al. 2015), which thrives on the principle of network effect (Hinz et al. 2020) (i.e., economic value = n^2, where n is the number of individuals enrolled on the platform) (Jiang et al. 2018). Same-side network effects occur when users directly benefit from new users' enrolment in a platform. In contrast, a cross-side network emerges when users of the original product increase not because of any direct benefit, but because of the effects of complementary products that lead to additional purchases.

According to Briscoe and Wilde (2006), digital ecosystems are distributed and open socio-technical systems where diverse entities compete or collaborate for resources and create value for different stakeholders (Briscoe and De Wilde 2006). Thus, their success depends upon positive value creation for all stakeholders. At the same time, malicious actors such as hackers and cybercriminals try to disrupt this value creation by executing cyberattacks and siphoning off customer data. It is observed that the presence of deterring entities such as cyber-insurers, legal authorities (such as FBI, Interpol), compliance structures (e.g., PCI-DSS, GSA), and robust perimeter security has helped to increase the customers on these platforms through positive network effects. In contrast, the presence of hackers results in negative network effects for gamers and citizens. The presence of many stakeholders like gamers and citizens attracts more hackers. But this, in turn, churns away the customers if there are too many malicious hackers. This thesis models the cyber-risk assessment, quantification, mitigation strategies for three multi-stakeholder digital ecosystems — online gaming platforms, smart cities, and crowdfunding platforms — using the concepts of data mining, machine learning, and econometrics methods. Figure 1.1 details three different digital ecosystems studies in this thesis and networks effects between various entities. Each digital ecosystem behaves like a two-sided platform populated by similar (e.g., gamers and citizens) or different (e.g., founders and funders) entities. The subsequent sections detail the workflow and network effects for each digital ecosystem.

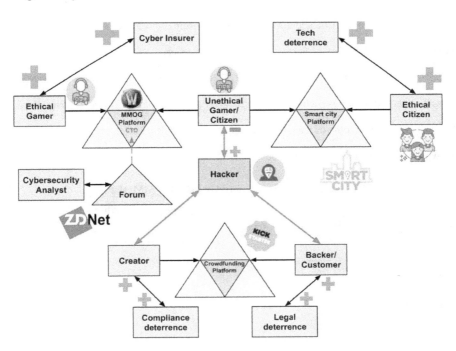

Figure 1.1 Overview of Digital Ecosystems

1.1.1. Massively Multiplayer Online Gaming (MMOG) platforms

Massively Multiplayer Online Games (MMOGs) and Role-Playing Games (MMORPG), such as Final Fantasy, World of Warcraft (WoW), Elder Scrolls, Star Wars Online, Guild Wars, Farmville, and PlayerUnknown's Battleground (PUBG), have emerged as popular entertainment options for young individuals with high disposable income (Wu and Hsu 2018). These MMOGs earn massive revenues for the game developers such as Blizzard, Nintendo, Ubisoft, Electronic Arts, and gaming platforms such as Steam, Twitch, PlayStation, and Xbox (Yahyavi and Kemme 2013). The global gaming market had a valuation of US$ 151.55 billion in 2019 and is forecasted to reach a value of US$ 256.97 billion by 2025 (MarketLine 2019). Analysts estimate that the global MMOG market will register a CAGR of 9.17% from 2020 to 2025. Euromonitor is optimistic about MMOG firms recording upwards of US$ 57 billion by 2024 (Euromonitor 2020). As of September 2020, Steam reached a user community strength of over 21 million concurrent users (Gough 2019). The early 2000s saw a steep rise in diverse gaming formats and offerings such as Box-to-play (B2P), Free-to-play (F2P), and Pay-to-play (P2P). Table 1.1 details some of the popular MMOG and MMORPG offerings over the years, along with their yearly revenue and number of subscribers.

Table 1.1: Data description of popular MMOG/ MMORPGs

Game name	Type	BTP	FTP	PTP	Monthly Fee (in US$)	Subscribers (in millions)	Yearly Revenue (in millions)
Ultima Online	B	—	—	Y	15	0.15	2.25
Dark Age of Camelot	B	—	—	Y	15	0.05	0.68
Final Fantasy XI	B	—	—	Y	15	0.50	7.50
Sims Online	A	—	Y	—	—	0.01	—

Game	Type	BTP/FTP		PTP	Subs.	Subscribers (millions)	Revenue (millions)
Eve Online	B	—	—	Y	15	0.23	3.45
Lineage 2	B	—	—	Y	15	1.00	15.00
Entropia Universe	A	—	Y	—	—	0.73	—
Second Life	A	—	Y	—	—	13.00	—
There	A	—	Y	—	—	2.00	—
City of Heroes	B	—	—	Y	15	0.13	1.88
Everquest 2	B	—	—	Y	15	0.20	3.00
World of Warcraft	B	—	—	Y	15	10.00	150.00
Guildwars	B	Y	—	—	20	4.40	88.00
Dungeons & Dragons	B	—	—	Y	15	0.05	0.75
Meez	A	—	Y	—	—	10.00	—
Tabula Rasa	B	—	—	Y	15	0.13	1.95
Vanguard	B	—	—	Y	15	0.04	0.60
Pirates of the Burning Sea	B	—	—	Y	15	0.08	1.13
Requiem	B	—	Y	—	—	0.70	—
Farmville	B	—	Y	—	—	—	—

BTP = Box-to-play, FTP=Free-to-play, PTP=Pay-to-play, Subs. = Subscription, A=MMOG, B=MMORPG

MMOG platforms offer various features such as teams and role-play to simulate real-life camaraderie, attracting many concurrent gamers (Yahyavi and Kemme 2013; Wu and Hsu 2018). First Person Shooter Games (FPS) and MMORPGs offer higher customizability owing to the fantasy-based storyline (e.g., Legend of Zelda, WoW) (Roquilly 2011). The MMOGs' low latency and high scalability significantly increase the game players' satisfaction and repeated purchase of in-game inventory, gizmos, level upgrades (Avinadav et al. 2020; Harviainen et al. 2020; Roquilly 2011). Some of the key stakeholders of the MMOG platforms are gamers, hackers, legal authorities, and cyber-insurers. Gamers have strong same-side network effects. While similar cross-side network effects are witnessed amongst gamers, legal authorities, and cyber-insurers. Contrary to this, we observe strong negative cross-side network effects between gamers and hackers, but it manifests positively the other way round. Thus, more gamers attract more hackers, but the converse is not valid. Figure 1.2 illustrates the varied interactions between different MMOG platform stakeholders, namely, gamers, hackers, and legal authorities (Freeman 1984; Samonas et al. 2020).

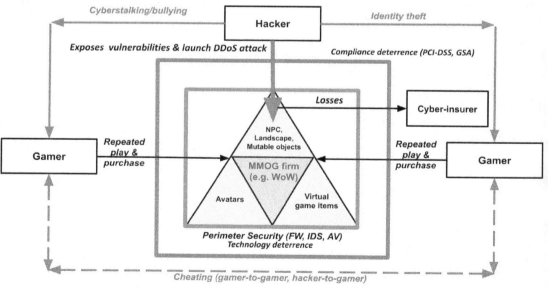

NPC = Non-player character, GSA = Gaming Standards Association
Figure 1.2: Stakeholders of an MMOG firm

Cyberattacks on MMOG platforms

As a result, black-hat hackers find MMOG platforms lucrative targets, where many gamers spend significant amounts of money. Hackers with low moral intensity and lack of fear of punishment tend to launch repeated cyberattacks (Ghoshal and Moran 1996; Mubako et al. 2020; Singhapakdi et al. 1996). Hackers also perceive higher behavioral control over their ability to cause harm. They think their technological prowess will make them untraceable (Chatterjee et al. 2015; Udo et al. 2016). Thus, they rationalize their unethical use with their subjective preference structure regarding cost, effort, and time (Becker 1978; Kahneman and Tversky 1979). Hackers compromise the "availability" components of the Confidentiality, Integrity, or Availability (CIA) triad by launching various Distributed-Denial-of-Service (DDoS) attacks (Whitman, 2004). DDoS attacks disrupt legitimate gamers' access to the MMOG platform (Fokker 2018). Also, some of them indulge in cyberstalking and cyberbullying to disrupt online platforms' civility and an individual's sense of safety (Dhillon and Smith 2019). Hackers install malicious botnets on unsuspecting gamers' systems and convert them into *'zombie'* machines. The *'zombies'* launch illegitimate traffic to a target machine, mixed with its usual data traffic. Recently, Mirai and Mariposa botnets have been popular amongst hackers (Gupta et al. 2012). These attacks reduce MMOG firms' latency and gamer experience, harm their reputation, and reduce perceived authenticity towards the gaming firm (Wu and Hsu 2018). Commonly, DDoS attacks used by hackers are as follows: Character Generation (CharGEN) attack, Network Time Protocol (NTP) Flood, User Datagram Protocol (UDP) Flood, UDP Fragment, Simple Service Discovery Protocol (SSDP) Flood, and DNS Flood (Peng et al. 2007a; Shani 2019). Table 1.2 lists the DDoS attack types, vulnerabilities exposed, intensity, and IT assets compromised in some recent attack incidents.

Table 1.2: DDoS variants and their characteristics

Attack	Route	CVE	CVSS	IT asset compromised			Incidents
				RS	LC	NW	
CharGEN	Peripheral devices, e.g., Game controller	1999-0103	5	–	Y	–	–
DNS Flood	DNS server	2009-0234	6	Y	–	–	Mirai DYN attack (2016)
NTP Flood	Network Time Protocol	2019-11331	7	Y	–	Y	–
SSDP Flood	Plug and play devices	2019-14323	5	–	Y	–	–
UDP Flood	UDP packets	2016-10229	10	Y	Y	–	Sony PS & Xbox (2014)

RS = Remote Server, LC = Local Client, NW = Network, VD = Vulnerability Detail, CVE = Common Vulnerabilities and Exposures, CVSS = Common Vulnerability Scoring System, CIA = Confidentiality, Availability, Integrity

Figure 1.3(a) shows that 74% of the DDoS attacks are aimed at the MMOG industry (McKeay 2017). While, figure 1.3(b) depicts a steep decrease in some popular games' yearly revenue, based on Table 1, as their service level decreases from 90% to 70% due to DDoS attacks.

The Chief Technology Officer (CTO) of an MMOG firm may resort to either accept, reduce, or pass the cyber-risk due to DDoS attacks (Mukhopadhyay et al. 2019). In most cases, they outsource to third-party services, easing the load on their in-house servers and helping scale with high service quality promise (Hui et al. 2012). MMOG firms also use scrubbing centers to isolate genuine traffic from the bulk and reduce cyber-risk incidences. In comparison, they might use third-party cyber-insurance policies to absorb the residual risk and resulting losses (Böhme 2005).

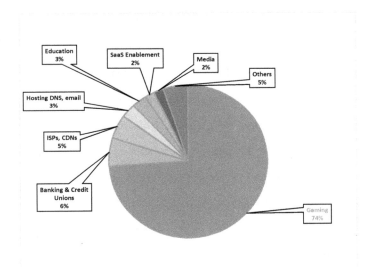

Figure 1.3(a): DDoS attacks on different industries (2018-2019)

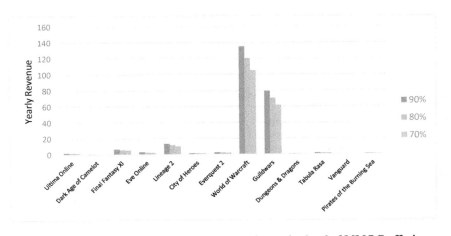

Figure 1.3(b): Revenue loss due to the decrease in service level of MMOG offerings

1.1.2. Smart cities

Smart cities are an integral part of the futuristic urban socio-economic ecosystem (Chen et al. 2021). Their success depends upon using digital technologies (such as mobile cloud computing, electronic objects, networks, sensors, and machine learning technologies), data, and design thinking to improve the effectiveness and efficiency of city services (Ismagilova et al. 2020; Solanki et al. 2019). One of the critical challenges in developing smart cities is processing and managing data (Chen et al. 2021; van Zoonen 2016). Unfortunately, cyber-attacks increased by 32% in 2018 due to increased Internet penetration. Hackers launch attacks every 39 seconds, on average 2244 times a day (Cukier 2007). The attack lifecycle can take as long as 314 days from breach to containment. At this rate, cyber-enabled ecosystems suffer from losses as significant as US$ 6 trillion by 2021 (Vecchio et al. 2019). Technology spending on smart city initiatives worldwide is forecast to more than double between 2018 and 2023, increasing from USD 81 billion in 2018 to USD 189.5 billion in 2023. Smart cities have frequently faced cyber-attacks (Pandey 2019). As shown in figure 1.4, we categorize different stakeholders in a smart city. The city administration is the chief service provider (Lom and Pribyl 2021; Ninčević Pašalić et al. 2021; Schulz et al. 2020), and citizens are service consumers. External actors such as legal and compliance authorities ensure the proper functioning of these services in physical and digital domains (Neumann et al. 2019). Malicious external actors such as cybercriminals disrupt smooth traffic functioning (Kim et al. 2021). For example, hackers may tamper with electronic speed limit signs. Autonomous vehicles employ computer vision to read electronic speed limit signs and adjust their maximum speed (González García et al. 2017). As a result, they may misread the speed limit, resulting in either collision or congestion on the pathways (Manfreda et al. 2021). We observe that the presence of hackers strengthens the negative cross-side network effects between them and citizens, thereby reducing their number. All other stakeholders have positive network effects.

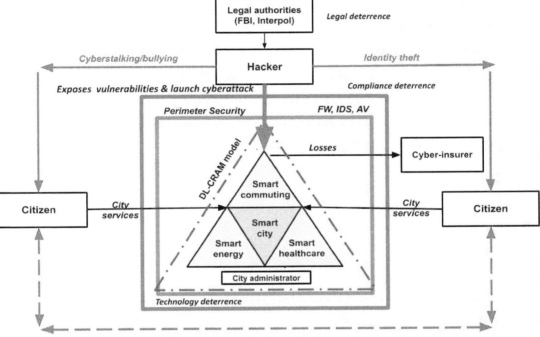

Figure 1.4: Stakeholders of a Smart city

Cyberattacks on smart cities

In 2020, McAfee manually tested Tesla Mobileye cameras on distorted road signs. In most cases, the camera system was easily compromised to read wrong or misleading information from street signs (Povolny and Trivedi 2020). A specific test case read 35 kmph as 85 kmph, thus seriously undermining self-driving systems and their use in smart cities. CityLab, a Bloomberg subsidiary, estimated that, on average, an American passenger/commuter lost US$ 2,000 per year due to traffic jams. Autonomous vehicles coupled with cyberattack-induced traffic anomalies can increase the losses to upward of US$ 19 billion for a city such as Los

Angeles (Schneider 2018). In 2019, the city of Baltimore came under a Ransomware attack that rendered its systems useless until a ransom was paid. Although the city paid US$ 76,280 to hackers, it is estimated that it lost US$ 18 million during the entire duration of the attack (Torbet 2020). In March 2018, Atlanta faced a cyberattack that resulted in US$ 10 million in losses by compromising poorly secured public computer systems (Sneed 2019). Table 1.3 summarizes the above cyberattacks on smart cities along with their estimated losses.

Table 1.3: Smart city attack incidents

Year	Smart city	Event	Losses (in billion USD)
2020	—	McAfee (Road sign distortion)	undetermined
2019	Baltimore city	—	0.001
2018	Los Angeles	Road Traffic	19.00
2018	Atlanta city	—	0.01
2018	Newark	—	0.001
2018	Sint Maarten	—	—

1.1.3. *Crowdfunding platforms*

Crowdfunding provides a new way for entrepreneurs to raise seed capital from a set of individuals rather than venture capitalists by posting their campaigns on the Internet. Founders of Pebble Watch collected a staggering seed capital (US$3.8 million) through the Kickstarter platform. Facebook's recent significant acquisition of Oculus VR started as a crowdfunding campaign that exceeded its US$250,000 funding goal within 24 hours, going on to raise over US$2.4 million. These are examples of the democratization of fund collection for entrepreneurs (Chang 2012; Mitchell 2014). Previously, entrepreneurs depended on venture capitalists (VCs) to raise their projects' funds. However, in most cases, the entrepreneur had to accede governance rights to the VC, such as an investor, which influenced the project's concepts, products design, and creativity, especially those related to arts and design (Aldrich 2014; Mollick and Nanda 2016). In recent times, crowdfunding campaigns ranged from goal amounts of US$100 to US$1 million. Quite recently, there has been a rise in crowdfunding activities on blockchain networks to overcome limitations such as security and immutability inherent in platform models (Tapscott 2016).

Crowdfunding is defined as an open call to gather financial resources from individual funders. These individual funders contribute to projects on various platforms (Schwienbacher and Larralde 2010). For example, Milap is a platform that has funders who donate for altruistic gains. While on Kickstarter, Indiegogo, GoFundMe, Ketto, individuals donate for reward or voting rights. Crowdfunding platforms have their origins in the concepts of micro-finance and crowd outsourcing activities. Online crowdfunding platforms are the most prominent and valuable due to increased ease of operations and help in reducing information asymmetry between founders and funders (Datta 2018).

Crowdfunding platforms can also be visualized as a two-sided market that comprises campaign "founders" and campaign "funders" on either side. They create value for founders in terms of the increased reach of their campaign idea, thus increasing its probability of it being funded. Most founders have limited networks of friends and relatives who may fund their innovative projects or ideas. However, through the cross-side network effect, these platforms help them connect to a large set of funders. Similarly, through the cross-side network effect, Funders have access to a set of curated innovative ideas or campaigns they can pledge funds for them. In turn, funders are rewarded by giving priority rights to a product post its launch or providing a discount on its purchase. Also, more funders will visit this platform through the same side network effect. The presence of strong same-side and cross-side network effects helps crowdsourcing platforms sustain themselves in the long run (Eisenmann et al. 2015; Parker et al. 2018). Figure 1.5 depicts the stakeholder view of crowdfunding platforms.

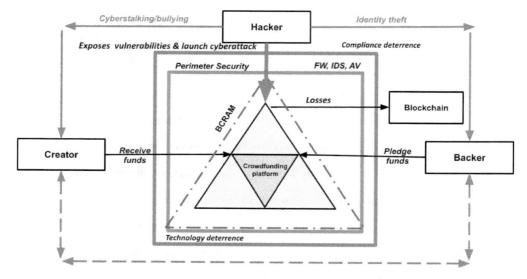

Figure 1.5: Stakeholder view of crowdfunding platforms

Fraudulent campaigns on crowdfunding platforms

Since its advent, crowdfunding platforms have been plagued by the proliferation of fraud campaigns. A substantial amount of incidents where Kickstarter had to cancel fraudulent campaigns have surfaced in recent times. Many highly successful campaigns such as Coolest Cooler had a massive backlog of orders. They charged expedited delivery fees to compensate for the lack of funds at the later product development phase, thus, raising questions about the ultimate success of such campaigns (Siering et al., 2016). Although frauds in reward-based crowdfunding are a quite rare phenomenon, it was reported by Kickscammed that more than 50% of projects do not deliver the promised rewards to backers, thereby totaling around US$ 3 million in fraudulent campaigns in the crowdfunding context. Still, these campaign founders have some common characteristics: they have rarely engaged in prior crowdfunding activities, have a weak social media presence, and provide less transparent and confusing campaign pitches (Cumming et al. 2016). Recently, researchers have observed instances of preemptive fraud, where founders cancel a successfully funded project before the campaign funds are transferred to them. This situation usually is "a consequence of a significant number of backer complaints to the platform provider, or numerous postings in forums or on blogs that the campaign carries a risk of fraud" (Cumming et al., 2016, p. 14).

1.2. Cyber-risk Management

Cyber-risk management has been at the helm of cybersecurity research since the advent of Newer Information Technology for businesses (Gordon et al. 2003). Cyber-risk management consists of three crucial steps: cyber-risk assessment, cyber-risk quantification, and cyber-risk mitigation.

Cyber risk assessment (CRA) methods intend to identify risky information assets (such as hardware and software systems, networks, customer data, and intellectual property) that cyber-attackers can attack. Thus, cyber-risk assessment aids in evaluating the efficacy of IT risk management compliance structure already in place in organizations. Information assets are divided into multiple classes according to the perceived risk in order of their severity and broken into sub-parts to correctly identify the risky component of the asset and its type (tangible and intangible) (O'Reilly et al. 2018; Smith and Eloff 2002). It also identifies vulnerable paths in the communication networks, which cyber-attackers can exploit to launch various attacks.

Cyber-risk quantification (CRQ) follows cyber-risk assessment and estimates the probability of identified risk with the help of diverse methods to attach a monetary value to it. Cyber risk quantification methods rely on the probability of a risky incident occurring and rigorous estimation of loss amount for such events. Thus, the accuracy of such techniques relies on thorough risk quantification and loss calculation. Loss estimation methods also evolve according to the unit of analysis and definition of loss for which we are undertaking the exercise, as mentioned earlier. Thus, the expected loss for entities resulting from cyberattacks depends not only on the incident but also on our ability to estimate its loss accurately. These estimations also vary in their methodological rigor depending upon the type and granularity of data available to calculate them. Cyber risk quantification techniques range from mathematical risk modeling to data mining methods using empirical data available from security providers (Campbell and Stamp 2004).

Cyber-risk mitigation (CRM), on the other hand, focusses on elucidating ways to reduce risk and severity arising due to compromise of risky assets by cyber-attackers. It considers subjective preferences and the risk appetite of the decision-maker to suggest interventions (financial as well as technological) to mitigate risk (Kahneman and Tversky 1979; Kunreuther 1997).

This thesis investigates three research questions. The first research question focuses on identifying risky assets in a cyber-enabled firm: cyber-risk assessment step. The second question tries to quantify cyber-risk by estimating the probability of cyber-risk occurrence. The third question investigates different ways of cyber-risk mitigation.

1.3. Thesis contributions

This thesis work has both academic as well as managerial implications across different studies grouped according to digital ecosystems. They are as described in the following sections.

1.3.1. Academic contributions

In this section, we list the academic contributions made through this thesis. We contribute across three digital ecosystems, ranging from identifying the value disruption to suggesting methods to quantify risk accurately. For the MMOG platforms, we contribute to the academic discussion by suggesting a novel predictor and framework for cyber-risk management in the MMOG industry. Our study contributes in the following ways. We treat cyber-risk management as a tool to reduce ethical concerns for MMOG firms emanating from hackers. Our study is one of the first studies to quantify and mitigate cyber-risk in MMO games using logit-probit, classification, and feedforward neural network models. The proposed model uses both attack-specific and MMOG platform-specific traits in quantifying cyber-risk. We use vulnerability trends as a proxy for cybersecurity spending. We assume that vulnerabilities will come down with more cybersecurity spending as then firms can invest more in coding best practices and team training. Lastly, we suggest cyber-insurance coupled with self-protection as a viable method to mitigate cyber-risk in the MMOG industry due to DDoS attacks.

While for smart cities, we identify the key stakeholders of a smart-city ecosystem (Israilidis et al. 2019) and model the workflows of the Integrated Traffic Management System (ITMS) and how hackers can disrupt them. First, we propose a time series and deep learning-based approach for smart cities' respective studies (Herath and Rao 2009; Lee et al. 2004). It is in line with the threat and coping appraisal components of Protection-Motivation Theory (PMT). Second, we devise risky scenarios of speed misinterpretation and sensor tampering along with risk and severity calculations. Within the DL-CRAM model, we use the Bayesian inference method (Hastie et al. 2009) to infer three risky scenarios emanating from hacker-induced manipulation (Awad et al. 2019). While SCRAM model uses SARIMA-based residual estimates to tag abnormal average speed records. We observed that our CRA module performed well in estimating probability values for such misreads. The final output from the CRA module computes the probability of detecting these speed limit misreadings and, subsequently, the expected loss caused by each. Our CRM module proposes perimeter security to deter hackers from resorting to speed limit disruption, as mentioned in the above risky scenarios (Lee et al. 2004). Additionally, we propose using financial mitigation strategies such as cyber-insurance policies (Kesan et al. 2013; Rejda 2007) to reduce the impact of such anomalies on the smart-city ecosystem (Manfreda et al. 2021).

Similarly, we contribute to the academic discourse through the study on crowdfunding platforms by suggesting a novel method of reducing the number of fraud campaigns by improving the campaign data quality and thereby boosting the accuracy with which the Kernel naïve Bayes classifier identifies the successful campaigns. Thus, crowdfunding platforms can onboard potentially successful campaigns and reduce failed campaigns.

1.3.2. Managerial implications

This section details the managerial contributions made through this thesis. We contribute by helping decision-makers prioritize risk mitigation strategies by investing in financial or technological interventions when they face cyberattacks. MMOG firms value latency, scalability, and brand reputation as revenue drivers. Our study has the following managerial implications. First, it provides CTOs with a tool with easy-to-understand steps and actionable cyber-risk management insights to mitigate DDoS attacks in the MMOG industry. The 2×2 cyber-risk mitigation heat-matrix provides exact mitigation steps and probable investment strategies. Thus, managers can gauge whether the firm needs to invest in technology, cyber-insurance, or both. These mitigation strategies will discourage the hackers from causing financial loss to the firm and increase customers' confidence in the authenticity of MMOG firms' offerings.

On the other hand, in case of smart cities, our models provide the city administrators with a heat matrix (i.e., of risk × severity) (Westerman and Hunter 2007), which details the different risky scenarios arising from hacker-induced speed limit sign manipulation. The city administrator can prioritize risk mitigation strategies (Böhme and Schwartz 2006, 2010; Kesan et al. 2013). As a result, the risk reduces; thereby, the administrator can self-insure (Rejda 2007). Subsequently, city administrators can pass the residual risk onto a third-party cyber insurer (Chatterjee et al. 2015; Kesan et al. 2005; Rejda 2007).

Similarly, in the case of crowdfunding platforms, it provides CTOs with a tool with easy-to-understand steps and actionable cyber-risk management insights to handle misclassification of campaigns as successful or failure. The 2×2 cyber-risk mitigation heat-matrix provides exact mitigation steps and probable investment strategies. Thus, managers could gauge whether the firm needs to invest in blockchain-based solutions, cyber-insurance, or both.

1.4. Organization of the thesis

The remainder of this thesis is organized as follows. The following section provides an overview of existing literature on cyber-risk management, MMOG platform, smart cities, and crowdfunding platforms. Chapter 3 explains the research questions, and Section 4 covers the methodology across the digital ecosystems. Chapter 5 describes the data used for the analysis, and Chapter 6 reports the empirical findings. Chapter 7 discusses the thesis' results, insights, future scope, and limitations. Finally, Chapter 8 concludes the thesis. As shown in figure 1.6, we study three digital ecosystems depending upon the components violated from the confidentiality-integrity-availability (CIA) triad. We observe that in MMOG platforms, hackers aim to disrupt the availability of cyber-resources to gamers, thereby resulting in increased latency and poor gaming experience. While smart cities suffer from integrity as well as availability issues brought forth by hackers attacking their smart systems such as Integrated Traffic Management Systems (ITMS). Malicious hackers target benign components such as speed sensors to disrupt traffic on smart city pathways. Lastly, we study crowdfunding platforms to explore the presence of fraudulent campaigns on them and resultant cyber-risk scenarios for these firms. We develop a cyber-risk management framework for the aforesaid platforms by assessing (CRA), quantifying (CRQ), and mitigating (CRM) risk, thus helping decision-makers accept, reduce, or pass cyber-risk entailed in business operations.

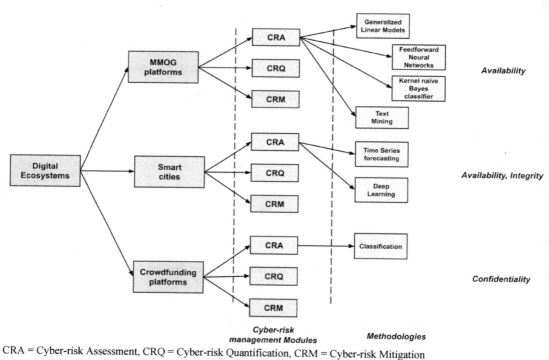

CRA = Cyber-risk Assessment, CRQ = Cyber-risk Quantification, CRM = Cyber-risk Mitigation

Figure 1.6: Broad overview of thesis in terms of methodologies used

2. Literature Review

This section details the extant literature and identifies research gaps pertaining to cyber-risk management across different digital ecosystems. We arrange the extant academic discussion around the different digital ecosystems through the cyber-risk management modules. Subsequently, we also elucidate the research gaps that motivate us to undertake this thesis. Figure 2.1 depicts the different heads under which the literature is grouped for further analysis.

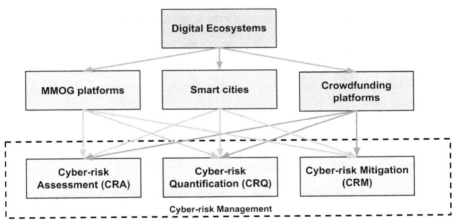

Figure 2.1: Broad overview of the literature in this thesis

2.1. Cyber-risk Management

Cyber-risk management has been a crucial activity in cybersecurity research since the advent of new and pervasive Information Technology for businesses (Gordon et al. 2003). According to Protection-Motivation theory (PMT) (Boss et al. 2015; Herath and Rao 2009; Rogers 1975), in case of fear appeal (i.e., cyberattacks in this context), a decision-maker should evaluate the likelihood as well as the severity of the aforesaid. Subsequently, they can choose between different strategies to reduce the frequency, severity, or both. It also follows from the Risk theory that process for cyber-risk management comprises three main activities. The first step entails cyber-risk assessment (CRA) where one estimates the likelihood of a cybersecurity breach followed by cyber-risk quantification (CRQ) to compute its impact. Lastly, the cyber-risk mitigation (CRM) stage uses the likelihood and the impact values for the aforesaid breach to inform subsequent strategies to mitigate the risk. Thus, the decision maker can decide between technological and financial interventions to reduce risk and severity (Bandyopadhyay and Mookerjee 2019; Biswas and Mukhopadhyay 2018; Courtney 1977; Mukhopadhyay et al. 2019; Sharma and Mukhopadhyay 2021a; Westerman and Hunter 2007). The subsequent sub-sections detail the literature across different cyber-risk management modules.

2.1.1. Cyber-risk Assessment (CRA)

The cyber-risk assessment process aims to analyze risky scenarios in a firm under cyber-attacks. These methods intend to identify information assets (such as hardware, software, customer data, and intellectual property) that are highly likely to cyber-attacks and resultant risks (Gordon et al. 2003; Nazareth & Choi 2015). Information assets are categorized into various classes according to the perceived risk and its severity and further divided into sub-parts to correctly attribute to the IT asset's risk profile (Baskerville et al., 2014; O'Reilly et al. 2018). The extant literature can be grouped under the various unit of analysis depending upon the components exploited by the hackers to breach the particular cyber-enabled systems. We observe that software bugs and system vulnerabilities provide backdoor access to hackers, thereby resulting in cyberattacks such as malware and network congestion. We also observe that probable mitigation strategies include proactive patching and honeypots to discourage hackers from compromising the systems. Table 2.1 details the cyber-risk assessment methods according to the unit of analysis.

Table 2.1 Cyber-risk Assessment methods

Year	Author	Unit of Analysis						
		Vuln.	Threat		Attack		Mitigation	
		V	C	M	A	N	P	H
2002	Anderson	Y	Y	—	—	—	—	—
2005	Rescorla	Y	—	—	—	—	—	—
2006	Alhazmi and Malaiya	Y	—	—	—	—	—	—
2008	Joh et al.	Y	—	—	—	—	—	—
2011	Woo et al.	Y	—	—	—	—	—	—
2011	Zhang et al.	Y	—	—	—	—	—	—
2012	Ransbotham et al.	Y	—	—	Y	—	—	—
2012	Nguyen and Massacci	Y	—	—	—	—	—	—
2013	Zhan et al.	—	—	—	—	—	—	Y
2014	Massacci and Nguyen	Y	—	—	—	—	—	—
2014	Zhan et al.	—	—	—	—	Y	—	—
2015	Mitra and Ransbotham	Y	—	—	Y	—	—	—
2015	Ruohonen et al.	Y	—	—	—	—	Y	—
2015	Roumani et al.	—	—	—	—	—	—	—
2016	Guo et al.	—	—	Y	—	—	—	—
2016	Huang et al.	Y	—	—	—	—	—	—

Year	Author							
2016	Younis et al.	—	Y	—	—	—	—	—
2016	Edwards et al.	—	—	—	—	—	—	—
2016	Johnson et al.	—	—	—	—	—	—	—
2016	Last	—	—	—	—	—	—	—
2016	Warkentin	—	Y	—	Y	—	—	—
2017	Munaiah et al.	Y	Y	—	—	—	—	—
2017	Stuckman et al.	—	Y	—	—	—	—	—
2017	Joh and Malaiya	Y	—	—	—	—	—	—
2017	Temizkan et al.	—	—	—	—	Y	—	—
2017	Yang et al.	—	—	—	Y	—	Y	—
2017	Hui et al.	—	—	—	Y	—	Y	—
2017	Wolff	Y	Y	—	Y	—	—	—
2017	Tang et al.	Y	—	—	—	—	—	—
2017	Sokol and Gajdoš	—	—	—	—	—	—	Y
2018	Samtani et al.	—	Y	—	—	—	—	—
2018	Biswas et al.	—	—	Y	—	—	—	—
2019	Das et al.	—	—	—	—	—	—	—
2019	Mukhopadhyay et al.	—	—	—	Y	—	—	—
2020	Zhang, Nan and Tan	—	—	—	Y	—	—	—
2020	Wang, Lu and Qin	—	—	—	—	Y	—	—

V = Vulnerabilities, C = Coding bugs, M = Malware, A = Attack, N = Network, P = Patches, H = Honeypot

2.1.2. Cyber-risk Quantification (CRQ)

Cyber-risk quantification module aims to evaluate the cyber-risk that have been identified followed by validating and analyzing them according to mathematical models that assign likelihood as well as loss values to the aforesaid. It helps the organizations heavily dependent on information technology to apportion their cybersecurity investment strategies and risk transfer decisions. We classify the extant cyber-risk quantification literature into two broad heads depending upon the use of structured or unstructured data to quantify risk. We observe that structured data uses data mining, fuzzy logic-based, and econometric methods, while unstructured has used text-mining extensively to quantify cyber-risk for firms. The subsequent sub-sections detail the aforesaid cyber-risk quantification methods. Figure 2.2 depicts the different subsections across this module.

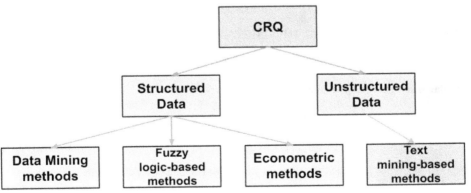

Figure 2.2: Overview of Cyber-risk Quantification (CRQ) methods

2.1.2.1. Structured Data

Data Mining Methods

Prior data mining methods have used datasets of past cyberattacks to model uncertain scenarios and to predict their likelihood (Biswas et al. 2018; Samtani et al. 2017; Wang et al. 2020). For instance, logit and probit models were used to estimate the probability of cyberattacks using CSI-FBI survey data from to 1997-2010 (Mukhopadhyay et al. 2019). Machine learning methods are best suited to assess cyber-risk due to cyberattacks employing social engineering strategies, such as phishing. The Bagger classifier and CART-based hybrid classifiers accomplish the same on the dataset of phishing URLs (Biswas and Mukhopadhyay 2017; Sharma and Mukhopadhyay 2020d). Text-mining methods to conduct cyber-threat intelligence have gained impetus due to the wide availability of log data and hacker-generated content (Jeyaraj and Zadeh 2020; Samtani et al. 2017; Sharma and Mukhopadhyay 2021; Wang, Ulmer, and Kannan 2013).

Rule-based methods, such as augmented decision tree classifiers, have been useful for analyzing cyberattacks from the CAIDA dataset (Balkanli et al. 2015). Prior studies' cyber-risk scenarios have also implemented density estimation techniques to augment methods depending on distribution statistics (Alhazmi et al. 2007).

Additionally, hybrid data mining methods (such as ensemble methods) are used to generate decision rules for classifying similar cyberattacks in the future. Generally, in complex scenarios such as cyberattacks, smaller feature vectors also result in a highly complex decision tree. Thus, the efficacy of these methods depends on the implementation of efficient pruning techniques (Biswas et al. 2016; Sharma and Mukhopadhyay 2020c).

Fuzzy Logic-based methods

Prior studies posit that fuzzy estimation of cyberattack probability results in better accuracy in cases where predictors are qualitative. Smith and Eloff (2002) have modeled the in-patient treatment process in a hospital using the cognitive-fuzzy method. They note that various technological assets are used to expose the system to cyberattacks and countermeasures deployed to reduce them. RiMaHCoF algorithm computes the risk at each sub-processes using the cognitive-fuzzy technique. Apart from cognitive-fuzzy methods, researchers have also employed fuzzy Analytical Hierarchal Process (AHP), and Rough sets to model such scenarios (Chimplee et al. 2006; Smith and Eloff 2002; Wu et al. 2009).

Econometric methods

Prior studies have used game theoretic models (Cavusoglu et al. 2008; Zhang, Nan and Tang 2020), Generalized Methods of Moments (Angst et al. 2017; D'arcy et al. 2020) and time-series modelling techniques such as GARCH (Biswas et al. 2017) to model cyberattacks along with vulnerabilities. Financial modelling methods such VaR (Bojanc and Blazic 2008; Qi et al. 2010) aid in estimating effects of cyberattacks wherein direct cyberattack is scarce. Further, copula-based methods have been used to quantify cyber-risk and suggest insurance approaches in complex cyber-risk scenarios (Herath and Herath 2011).

Table 2.2 summarizes the literature on cyber-risk quantification.

Table 2.2: Cyber-risk Quantification methods

Year	Authors	Qualitative	Empirical			Mixed method
			DM	FL	E/S	
2020	Zhang, Nan and Tan	–	–	–	Y	–
	Wang, Lu and Qin	–	Y	–	–	–
2019	Das et al.	–	Y	–	–	–
	Mukhopadhyay et al.	–	Y	–	–	–
2018	Samtani et al.	–	Y	–	–	–
	Biswas et al.	–	Y	–	–	–
2017	Biswas et al.	–	–	–	Y	–
2015	Balkanli et al.	–	Y	–		–
2010	Qi et al.	–	–	–	Y	–
	Zhang et al.	–	–	–	–	Y
2009	Pak et al.	–	Y	–	–	–
	Wu et al.	–	–	Y	–	–
2008	Cavusoglu et al.	–	–	–	Y	–
	Bojanc and Blazic	–	–	–	Y	–
	Srivastava et al.	–	Y	–		–
2007	Alhazmi et al.	–	–	–	Y	–
	Herath et al.	–	–	–	Y	–

Year	Author					
2006	Smith and Eloff	–	–	Y	–	–
	Chimplee et al.	–	–	Y	–	–
	Arnes et al.	–	Y	–	–	–
	Dhillon and Blackhouse	–	–	–	–	Y
2005	Kabacak and Sogukpinar	Y	–	–	Y	–
2004	Cavusoglu et al.	–	–	–	–	–
2003	CCC	Y	–	–	–	–
2002	Dorofee and Alberts	Y	–	–	–	–
	Stolen et al.	Y	–	–	–	–
	SANS Institute	Y	–	–	–	–
	Gordon and Loeb	–	–	–	Y	–
2001	Jaisingh et al.	–	–	–	Y	–
2000	Dhillon and Blackhouse	–	Y	–	–	Y
1993	Baskerville	–	–	–	–	Y
1988	CSC	–	–	–	–	Y
1981	Parker	Y	–	–	–	–

DM = Data Mining, FL = Fuzzy Logic, E/S = Econometric and Statistical

2.1.2.2. Unstructured Data

Text mining methods

Recently, many cybersecurity-related digital trace data has been discovered in the form of textual logs, hacker forum discussions, and public sentiment from social networking sites (Yue et al. 2019). Thus, it becomes imperative to analyze text mining methods as appropriate ways to extract themes and quantify the likelihood of attacks in conjunction with insights from the text. Table 2.3 details the use of text mining algorithms in cybersecurity literature.

Table 2.3: Text mining in Cybersecurity literature

Authors	Year	Dataset		Classification algorithms					Security components			
		C	P	DT	EN	SVM	NN	Others	T	A	C	I
Narouei et al.	2020	Y	—	—	—	Y	—	—	—	—	Y	—
Pellet et al.	2019	Y	—	—	—	—	—	Y	Y	—	—	—
Yu et al.	2019	—	Y	—	—	—	Y	—	Y	—	—	—
Noor et al.	2019	—	Y	—	—	—	—	Y	—	Y	—	—
Adewole et al.	2019	—	—	—	—	—	—	Y	—	—	Y	—
Fang et al.	2019	Y	—	—	—	—	—	Y	—	—	—	Y
Phan & Zincir-Heywood	2019	—	Y	—	—	—	Y	—	—	—	—	Y
Abuhamad et al.	2019	Y	—	—	—	—	Y	—	—	—	—	Y
Shao et al.	2019	Y	—	—	—	Y	—	—	—	—	—	Y
An and Kim	2018	Y	—	—	—	—	—	Y	Y	—	—	—

Author	Year											
Kudugunta and Ferrara	2018	Y	—	—	Y	—	—	—	Y	—	—	—
Aldwairi and Alwahedi	2018	Y	—	—	—	—	—	Y	—	Y	—	—
Park et al.	2018	—	Y	—	—	—	—	Y	—	Y	—	—
Toor et al.	2018	Y	—	—	—	—	Y	—	—	—	Y	—
Huang et al.	2018	—	Y	—	—	—	—	Y	—	—	Y	—
Deliu et al.	2017	Y	—	—	—	Y	—	—	Y	—	—	—
Vidros et al.	2017	—	Y	—	Y	—	—	—	Y	—	—	—
Edwards et al.	2017	Y	—	Y	—	—	—	—	—	Y	—	—
Rout et al.	2017	Y	—	—	—	—	—	—	—	—	Y	—
Milosevic et al.	2017	—	Y	—	—	—	—	—	—	—	Y	—
Suleiman and Al-Naymat	2017	—	—	—	—	—	—	Y	—	—	Y	—
Li et al.	2017	Y	—	Y	—	—	—	—	—	—	—	Y
Li et al.	2016	Y	—	—	—	Y	—	—	Y	—	—	—
El-Alfy and AlHasan	2016	—	—	—	—	—	—	Y	—	—	Y	—
Moghimi and Varjani	2016	Y	—	—	—	Y	—	—	—	—	Y	—
Zardari and Jung	2016	Y	—	—	—	—	Y	—	—	—	Y	—
Huang et al.	2016	Y	—	—	—	—	—	Y	—	—	—	Y
Srinandhini and Sheeba	2015	Y	—	—	—	—	—	—	Y	—	—	—
Slankas et al.	2014	Y	—	—	—	—	—	Y	—	—	Y	—
Zitar and Hamdan	2013	—	Y	—	—	—	Y	—	—	—	Y	—

Alneyadi et al.	2013	Y	—	—	—	—	—	Y	—	—	Y	—
Wang et al.	2013	Y	—	—	—	—	—	—	—	—	—	Y

C = Custom, P = Proprietary, DT = Decision Tree, EN = Ensemble, SVM = Support Vector Machine, NN= Neural Networks, T = Threat, A = Attack, C = Controls, I = Incidents

2.1.3. Cyber-risk Mitigation (CRM)

The last step of the cyber-risk management process involves suggesting ways to mitigate the risk, given the probability and impact of cybersecurity breaches. Researchers have suggested technological and financial interventions to mitigate cyber-risks (Bojanc & Jerman-Blažič, 2008). Technological interventions have focused on vulnerability assessment (Hoffman et al. 1978; Mukhopadhyay et al. 2007; Ozier 1989), threat identification (Baskerville 1993; Guarro 1987; Ozier 1989), design of security protocols (Mukhopadhyay et al. 2019), and controls (Guarro 1987). On the other hand, financial interventions have dealt with cyber-insurance as a tool to deter hackers and strengthen a firm's security attitude and mitigate cyber-risks (Böhme and Kataria 2006; Böhme and Schwartz 2010; Kesan et al. 2013; Majuca et al. 2006). Tables 2.4 categorizes the cyber-risk mitigation-related technological interventions according to vulnerability assessment, threat identification, security measures, and controls entailed in them.

Table 2.4: Cyber-risk mitigation through technological interventions

Authors	Year	VA	TI	SM	CN
Roumani	2022	–	Y	–	–
Chen et al.	2022	–	–	Y	–
Sharma and Mukhopadhyay	2022	Y	–	Y	–
Schmitz et al.	2021	–	–	Y	Y
Biswas et al.	2021	Y	–	Y	–

Author	Year	VA	TI	SM	CN
Ahmed et al.	2021	Y	–	–	–
Xu and Warkentin	2020	–	–	Y	Y
Rostami et al.	2020	–	–	Y	–
Mukhopadhyay et al.	2019	–	–	Y	–
Yue et al	2019	–	Y	Y	–
Das et al.	2019	–	Y	Y	–
Verkijika	2018	–	–	Y	–
Yilmaz and Gonen	2018	–	Y	–	–
Biswas et al	2017	–	–	Y	Y
Hubbard and Seierse	2016	–	–	–	Y
He and Zhan	2013	–	–	Y	Y
Bulgurcu et al	2010	–	–	–	Y
Mukhopadhyay et al.	2007	Y	–	–	–
Baskerville	1993	–	Y	Y	–
Ozier	1989	Y	Y	Y	–
Guarrao	1987	–	Y	–	Y
Hoffman et al.	1978	Y	–	–	–

VA: Vulnerability assessment, TI: Threat identification, SM: Security measures, CN: Controls

As recorded in table 2.5, we categorize financial interventions pertaining to cyber-risk mitigation according to their economic, financial impacts and whether they follow a game-theoretic or utility-based approach.

Table 2.5: Cyber-risk mitigation through financial interventions

Authors	Year	EI	FI	UT	GT
Masuch et al.	2022	–	Y	–	–
Chen et al.	2022	–	–	Y	–
Sharma and Mukhopadhyay	2022	–	Y	–	–
Vedadi et al.	2021	–	–	Y	Y
Zhang et al.	2021	Y	Y	–	–
Biswas et al.	2021	Y	–	–	–
Tripathi and Mukhopadhyay	2021	–	Y	–	–
Zhang, Naan and Tan	2020	–	–	–	Y
Milosavic et al.	2019	Y	–	Y	–
Das et al.	2019	Y	Y	–	–
Navarro et al.	2018	–	Y	–	–
Bohme and Schwartz	2010	–	–	Y	–
Ko et al.	2006	–	Y	–	–
Bohme and Kataria	2006	–	–	Y	–
Kesan and Majuca	2005	–	–	Y	–
Cashell	2004	Y	–	–	–

EI: Economic impact of cyberattacks, FI: Financial impact on firm performance, UT: Utility-based approach, GT: Game-theoretic approach

2.2. Digital Ecosystems

2.2.1. Massively Multiplayer Online Gaming (MMOG) platforms

MMOGs have millions of users concurrently producing massive network traffic and overhead processing loads for gaming (Wu and Hsu 2018). To provide a seamless and authentic gaming experience to users, MMOG firms need to address the following issues:(a) scalability, that is, provisioning game-play to millions of users concurrently, (b) consistency, (c) security, and (d) fast response time, or all of these collectively. In the absence of any of these, customer satisfaction suffers (Yahyavi and Kemme 2013). Thus, the game's availability to end-users is desirable (Liu et al. 2013). On these MMOG platforms, gamers regularly play, conduct financial transactions, and virtual currency exchange, thus, transforming it into an opportunity to cause disruptions (Huang et al. 2020). Distributed Denial-of-Service (DDoS) attacks are used as smoke-screens by attackers to divert MMOG firms' attention and siphon off gamers' records (Yue et al. 2019).

Gamers simulate real-life camaraderie through various game features such as teams, role-play, etc., on MMOG platforms (Yahyavi and Kemme 2013). These MMO games transport them to virtual worlds, economies, and fantasy lands (Wu and Hsu 2018). MMOGs include scenarios with multi-players teams trying to accomplish a coveted goal (Yahyavi and Kemme 2013). First Person Shooter Games (FPS) such as Counterstrike, PUBG, etc., enable end-users to don the avatar of a stealth fighter with shooting weapons and ammunition (Fu et al. 2017). Role-playing variants of MMOGs (MMORPGs) offer higher customizability owing to the fantasy-based storyline (e.g., Legend of Zelda, WoW, etc.) (Roquilly 2011). The MMOGs' low latency and high scalability significantly increase the game players' satisfaction and repeated purchase of in-game inventory, gizmos, level upgrades, etc. Most of these games follow the free-to-play model, and thus, in-game purchases form a chief source of revenue (Avinadav et al. 2020; Roquilly 2011).

MMOG firms deploy skilled and creative game developers to outsmart their competitors. Most of the gamers prefer value-for-money and thus, switch to newer and varied games quite often. Aesthetic design, customizability, healthy community, and co-creation opportunities play an important role in retaining gamers in a particular game (Wu and Hsu 2018). Gaming firms like Nintendo constantly innovate to add new players and prevent customer churn (Hyeong et al. 2020). Unlike the traditional platform business model, network effects do not play a significant role in MMOGs (Kanat et al. 2018; Yahyavi and Kemme 2013). Game-play quality (i.e., aesthetic design, avatars, landscape, non-mutable objects, etc.) significantly influences gamers' switching behavior (Messinger et al. 2009). Researchers have also observed that online game communities form organically as the game's popularity rises. Thus, gaming forums positively affect co-creation and customer acquisition (Zhang et al. 2019).

2.2.2. Smart cities

"Smart-city," as a concept, abstracts the use of technology-based solutions to improve citizens' lives and mediate their interaction with government and other citizens (Chourabi et al. 2012; Ben Yahia et al. 2019; Yu and Xu 2018). Smart cities use data collected through sensors to automate various services to improve performance, lower costs, or reduce environmental impacts (Alsop 2021). This literature can be grouped under operational issues and areas detrimental to the success of smart cities, such as cybersecurity and privacy (Chatterjee et al. 2019; Deakin 2013; Elmaghraby and Losavio 2014; Yeh 2017). Cybersecurity issues in smart cities can be grouped under three heads: (i) operational threats in diverse scenarios, such as smart homes, smart healthcare, smart transit, etc., (ii) security and privacy frameworks, and (iii) government initiatives and social media coercion which reduces the transaction cost associated with mobilizing citizens about cybercrime prevention (Albino et al. 2015; Janssen et al. 2019; Kar et al. 2019; Langley et al. 2021; Lom and Pribyl 2021; Mamonov and Koufaris 2020; Manfreda et al. 2021; Yeh 2017). Studies have also been conducted on the behavioral perception of digital technologies in the context of city services. A prominent research gap exists in estimating cyber risk from empirical evidence and elucidating the probable mediating channel—table 2.6 details the cybersecurity issues in smart cities grouped according to CIA violations.

Table 2.6: Cybersecurity issues in smart cities

Year	Authors	C	I	A	Year	Authors	C	I	A
2019	Gheisariy et al.	Y	—	—	2017	Antonopoulos et al.	Y	—	Y
2019	Han et al.	—	Y	—	2017	Beltran et al.	Y	—	—
2019	Huerta and Salazar	—	Y	—	2017	Lai et al.	—	—	Y
2019	Khedr et al.	Y	—	—	2017	Beltran et al.	Y	—	—
2019	Krichen and Alroobaea	—	Y	—	2017	de Fuentes et al.			
2019	Peters et al.	—	—	Y	2017	Ferdowsi et al.			
2019	Roldan et al.	—	Y	—	2017	González García et al.	—	Y	—
2019	Berg et al.	Y	—	—	2017	Guo et al.	Y		—
2019	Xie and Hwang	Y	—	—	2017	Luo et al.	Y	Y	—
2019	Yilei and Leyou	Y	—	—	2017	Shen et al.		Y	—
2018	Al-Dhubhani et al.	Y	—	—	2017	Song et al.	Y	—	—
2018	Gope et al.	Y	—	—	2017	Xiao et al.	Y	—	—
2018	Stromire and Potoczny-Jones	Y	—	—	2017	Zang et al.	Y	—	—
2018	Sucasas et al.	Y	—	—	2016	Avgerou et al.	Y	—	—
2018	Wibowo	—	Y	—	2016	Lepinski et al.	—	Y	—
2018	Witti and Konstantas	—	Y	—	2016	Mazhelis et al.	—	Y	—
2017	Antonopoulos et al.	Y	—	—	2015	Burange and Misalkar	Y	—	—

2017	Beltran et al.	Y	—	Y	2015	Cagliero et al.	Y	—	—
2017	Lai et al.	—	—	—	2015	Patsakis et al.	Y	—	—
2017	Beltran et al.	Y	—	Y	2013	Sen et al.	—	—	Y
2017	de Fuentes et al.				2017	Antonopoulos et al.	Y	—	Y
2018	Witti and Konstantas	—	Y	—					

C = Confidentiality, I = Integrity, A = Authenticity

2.2.3. Crowdfunding platforms

Crowdfunding platforms can also be visualized as a two-sided market that comprises campaign "founders" and campaign "funders" on either side. They create value for founders in terms of the increased reach of their campaign idea, thus increasing its probability of it being funded. Most founders have limited networks of friends and relatives who may fund their innovative projects or ideas. However, through the cross-side network effect, these platforms help them connect to a large set of funders. Similarly, through the cross-side network effect, Funders have access to a set of curated innovative ideas or campaigns they can pledge funds for them. In turn, founders are rewarded by giving priority rights to a product post its launch or providing a discount on its purchase. Also, more funders will visit this platform through the same side network effect. The presence of strong same-side and cross-side network effects helps crowdsourcing platforms sustain themselves in the long run (Eisenmann et al. 2015; Parker et al. 2018).

3. Research questions

This section formulates the research questions for undertaking cyber-risk management decisions for three digital ecosystems across studies. According to Protection-Motivation theory, any fear appeal (e.g., cyberattacks) can be evaluated by two processes, namely, threat appraisal and coping appraisal. Threat appraisal entails estimating the likelihood of fear appeal and the severity of its impact. On the contrary, coping appraisal mechanisms enlist different strategies to mitigate the fear-inducing event. We formulate three major research questions across studies related to three digital ecosystems. These research questions also correspond to three main modules, following from Risk theory (Kleindorfer and Kunreuther 1999) — Cyber-risk assessment (CRA), Cyber-risk Quantification (CRQ), and Cyber-risk mitigation (CRM). Figure 3.1 depicts the aforesaid relationships between cyber-risk management modules across digital ecosystems.

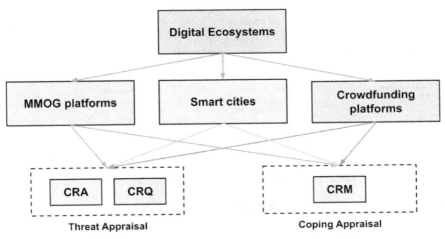

Figure 3.1: Overview of studies in terms of cyber-risk management modules

3.1. Massively Multiplayer Online Gaming (MMOG) platforms

We formulate the research questions and model for the MMOG platforms following a process-view of firm's response in case of cyberattacks (such as DDoS attacks). We observe that firms can only decide based on attack intensity and duration immediately after a cyberattack. It gives them an approximate idea of the likelihood and severity of attacks. Firms conduct cybersecurity forensics to identify critical vulnerabilities that need to be patched to increase predictive accuracy to prevent future cyberattacks. It is also observed that cybersecurity agencies (such as CERT and MITRE) take two quarters to reveal the vulnerabilities. Thus, vulnerability data of current and previous quarters play an essential role in predicting the likelihood of attacks. Therefore, we propose three frameworks related to posthoc analysis of likelihood using attack and vulnerability data. Similarly, we also propose a proactive approach to measuring the cyber-risk due to decision-makers' misinterpretation of cyber attack-related information. As shown in figure 3.2, the studies according to the process-view approach can be grouped pre-attack and post-attack.

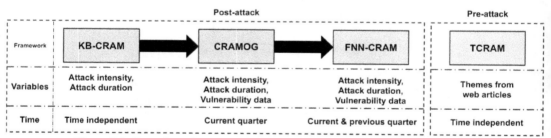

Figure 3.2: Overview of the process-view approach for MMOG-related studies

3.1.1. Kernel naïve Bayes classifier-based cyber-risk assessment and mitigation framework for online gaming platforms (KB-CRAM)

In this study, we model MMOG firms' cyber-risk of being the target of DDoS attacks; for this purpose, we adopt a process view approach (Rogers 1975). Our proposed KB-CRAM model, as shown in Figure 3.3, was developed based on protection motivation theory (PMT) (Rogers 1975; Boss et al. 2015; Bulgurcu, Cavusoglu, and Benbasat 2010), and it consists of three modules. The first module deals with cyber-risk assessment and calculates the probability of occurrence of a DDoS attack. Subsequently, cyber-risk quantification modules estimate the magnitude of the impact of these DDoS attacks, while cyber-risk mitigation helps the CTO choose the most effective protective response.

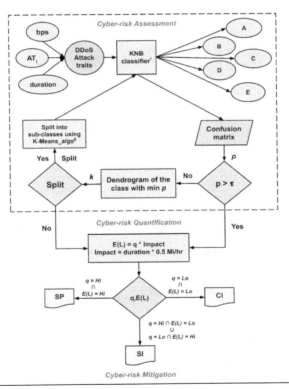

AT = Attack type; Attack class labels = A, B, C, D, E; q = (1-p) = Misclassification rate; p = Overall model accuracy; τ = Accuracy threshold; k = optimal number of clusters; SP = Self-protection; SI = Self-insurance; CI = Cyber-insurance, *Classification, #Clustering

Figure 3.3 Proposed Model for KB-CRAM

3.1.1.1. Cyber-risk Assessment (CRA)

In this module, there are two sub-stages. As shown in table 3.1, a hacker can launch a DDoS attack belonging to five attack classes using six different attack types.

Table 3.1: Relationship between DDoS attack class and DDoS attack types

DDoS Attack Class	AT_1	AT_2	AT_3	AT_4	AT_5	AT_6
A	Y	Y	—	—	—	—
B	—	—	Y	—	—	—
C	Y	—	—	Y	—	—
D	—	—	—	—	Y	—
E	—	—	—	—	—	Y

AT_1: UDP Fragment, AT_2: DNS Flood; AT_3: NTP Flood; AT_4: CharGEN Attack; AT_5: SSDP Flood; AT_6: UDP Flood

The DDoS attacks adversely slow down the operations of an MMOG firm if the intensity of illegitimate traffic (bps) and its duration (duration) is high (Cavusoglu et al. 2008; Sharma and Mukhopadhyay 2020; Yue et al. 2019). Table 3.2 details the relevant literature support for the choice of the variables.

Table 3.2: Model variables and relevant literature support

Variable name	Variable symbol	Literature
Attack type	Attack type	(McKeay 2017; Peng et al. 2007; Wang et al. 2020)
Attack intensity	bps	(Peng et al. 2007; Tanenbaum and Wetherall 2010; Wang et al. 2020; Zhang et al. 2020)

Attack duration	duration	(Peng et al. 2007; Tanenbaum and Wetherall 2010; Wang et al. 2020; Zhang et al. 2020)
Probability of attack for MMOG	p	(Biswas et al. 2017; Biswas and Mukhopadhyay 2018; Das et al. 2019; Mukhopadhyay et al. 2019)

In this context, we propose the following research question:

RQ1: What is the best estimation of the DDoS attack detection probability for MMOG firms?

Equation 1 shows the mathematical representation of our kernel naïve Bayes-based classifier, where AT_i is attack types.

$$p = P(C_i = A, B, C, D, E \mid X = bps, duration, AT_1, AT_2, \ldots, AT_7)$$

$$p = \frac{P(X|C_i) \times P(C_i)}{P(X)} \quad (1)$$

3.1.1.2. Cyber-risk Quantification (CRQ)

Next, we quantify the expected financial losses resulting from each type of DDoS attack in the MMOG industry. According to a Neustar report, a firm loses USD $0.5 million per hour during a DDoS attack (Bezsonoff 2017; Sharma and Mukhopadhyay 2020b, 2020a; Tripathi and Mukhopadhyay 2020). We use this information to calculate the expected loss (E[L]), that is, the product of the probability of misclassifying the DDoS attack with the loss incurred due to the DDoS attack (Campbell et al. 2003).

RQ2: What is the expected loss due to each type of DDoS attack on MMOG firms?

We calculate the expected loss as shown in Equations 2 and 3 (Courtney 1977), where q is the probability of misclassifying the DDoS attack:

$$E(L) = q \times Impact \tag{2}$$

$$Impact = (duration\ of\ DDoS\ attack) \times (0.5\ million\ loss\ per\ hour) \tag{3}$$

3.1.1.3. Cyber-risk Mitigation (CRM)

The proposed model's final stage pertains to cyber-risk mitigation; in this stage, we suggest ways to reduce the risk and severity of DDoS attacks in the MMOG industry. The risk values (probability of attack) and severity values (expected loss) serve as the module's primary inputs. According to Rational choice theory (Becker 1990; McCarthy 2002), a decision-maker weighs the costs and benefits of diverse choices, choosing whichever option is most closely aligned with their subjective preference structure. Similarly, CTOs are concerned with reducing risk as well as severity, thus, modeling the utility of both these choices becomes necessary. They consider the firm's risk profile and decide which are the appropriate technological and financial interventions to reduce (self-protection), accept (self-insurance), or transfer (cyber-insurance) risk (Böhme 2005; Böhme and Schwartz 2006; Kesan et al. 2013; Majuca et al. 2006).

RQ3: What cyber-risk mitigation strategies should CTOs use for each type of DDoS attack on MMOG firms?

3.1.2. A logit-based Cyber-risk Assessment and Mitigation model for Massively Multiplayer Online Gaming (CRAMOG) platforms

Following the previous section, we add the vulnerability of the current quarter to the analysis to improve the predictive accuracy of the model. According to the opportunity theory of crime, the hacker exploits vulnerabilities in the cyber-enabled firm with minimal or security controls (Cohen and Felson 1979). On the other hand, the CTOs of the firms resort to a layered approach towards fear appeals originating from cyber-attacks (Schneier 2001). The CTO assesses the probability of the cyberattack and the magnitude of its impact on them. Based on these, they enlist their protective responses (Boss et al. 2015; Bulgurcu et al. 2010; Rogers 1975). Also, decision-makers (CTOs) use rational choice theory to choose the best protective response according to cost-benefit analysis (Becker 1990; McCarthy 2002). The process of cyber-risk management closely follows from risk theory (Kunreuther 1997). It states that uncertain scenarios need to be dealt with risk assessment, quantification followed by mitigation by weighing costs and benefits. Based on the discussion above, our proposed CRAMOG model consists of three modules – Cyber-risk Assessment, Cyber-risk Quantification, and Cyber-mitigation for an MMOG firm, as shown in figure 3.4.

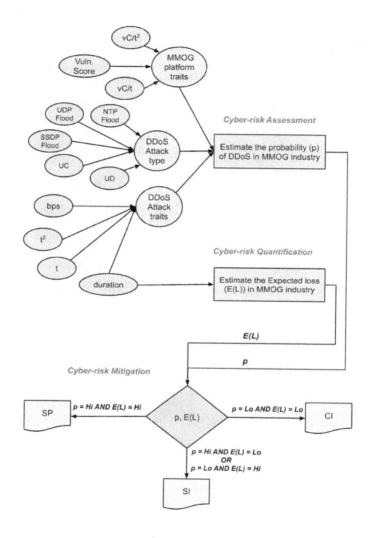

vC = Vulnerability count, t = Time, SP = Self-protection, SI = Self-insurance, CI = Cyber-insurance, Vuln. = Vulnerability, bps = bits per second, UC = UDP Fragment + CharGen, UD = UDP Fragment + DNS Flood

Figure 3.4: Proposed model for CRAMOG framework

3.1.2.1. Cyber-risk Assessment (CRA)

Hackers are classified into black hat (or unethical) hackers and white hat (or ethical) hackers based on their behavioral motivations (Smith 2002). White-hat hackers follow rule-based ethics and use their technical prowess to fix vulnerabilities and help firms proactively secure their customers against malicious attacks ((Chan & Janjarasjit, 2019; Chatterjee et al. 2015; Kant 1959; Kant and Korsgaard 1998). On the other hand, black-hat hackers' behavior can be explained using the consequentialist philosophy as their actions are based on financial or social utility gains (Chatterjee et al. 2015; D'Arcy et al. 2020; Heimo et al. 2018). They also weigh their benefits compared to costs in terms of effort, time, and punishments, as explained by the opportunity theory of crime (Cohen and Felson 1979; Eccles and Williamson 1987). They also display high technological relativism and low technological idealism (Banerjee et al. 1998; Barnett et al. 1994; Chatterjee et al. 2015; Forsyth 1980; Reidenbach et al. 1991).

Black-hat hackers tend to exploit inherent vulnerabilities in MMOG platforms to launch a DDoS attack to slow down the overall gaming experience for end-users. This reduced experience leads to customer attrition (Arora et al. 2008; Biswas et al. 2016; Das et al. 2019; Kannan and Telang 2005; Ransbotham et al. 2012; Peng et al. 2007b; Tripathi and Mukhopadhyay 2020). The probability (p_t) of a DDoS attack increases till the time (t, t^2) zero-day vulnerabilities are not patched in software used by MMOG firms (Mukhopadhyay et al. 2019; Wang et al. 2020). The computer emergency response team (CERT) takes approximately six months to publicly disclose a vulnerability discovered in a technology vendor's code (Ransbotham et al. 2012). CERT and MITRE announce the vulnerability score (CVSS) to convey their severity to the technology vendors. As a result, the technology vendors focus on creating security patches for vulnerabilities with the highest severity scores (i.e., vscr) (Arora et al. 2008; Kannan and Telang 2005). This will reduce the probability (p_t) of DDoS attacks on an MMOG platform (Biswas et al. 2016; Cavusoglu et al. 2008; Das et al. 2019; Peng et al. 2007; Tripathi and Mukhopadhyay 2020). The overall vulnerabilities (vC/t and vC/t^2) of the MMOG platform tend to come down as they deploy the respective patches from the technology vendors (Cavusoglu et al. 2008). Moreover, the MMOG firms will increase security defenses (e.g., firewalls, cyber-insurance), train staff in best practices, design mitigation plans, and develop frameworks for bug-free software products (Angst et al. 2017; Cavusoglu et al. 2008).

They tend to launch DDOS attacks on the MMOG platforms using these vulnerabilities. The DDoS attacks adversely slow down the operations of an MMOG firm if the intensity of illegitimate traffic (bps) and its duration (duration) is high (Cavusoglu et al. 2008; Sharma and Mukhopadhyay 2020; Yue et al. 2019).

As shown in Equations 3 and 4, we use the Generalized Linear Model (GLM) (McCullagh and Nelder 1989) to estimate the probability (p) of five kinds of DDoS attacks (i.e., NTPFLood, UDPflood, SSDPFlood, UC, UD) using the predictors mentioned earlier. Our model uses link functions such as M1 and M2 to estimate the probability of a DDoS attack using an exponential function (McCullagh and Nelder 1989; Mukhopadhyay et al. 2019).

RQ1a: What is the probability (p) of DDoS attacks on MMOG firms?

M1		M2	
$p_{type} = \dfrac{1}{1+e^{-Z_i}}$ (3)		$p_{type} = \Phi^{-1}(Z_i)$ (4)	

where $Z_i = \beta_0 + \beta_1 bps + \beta_2 duration + \beta_3 t + \beta_4 t^2 + \beta_5 vulnScore + \beta_6 \dfrac{vC}{t} + \beta_7 \dfrac{vC}{t^2}$

p$_{type}$ = probability of DDoS attack, type = NTPFlod, UDPFlod, SSDPFlood, UC, UD

Next, we also test whether the probability of DDoS attacks follows the beta distribution (Hossack et al. 1983).

RQ1b: What is the probability distribution of the probability of DDoS attacks on MMOG firms?

3.1.2.2. Cyber-risk Quantification (CRQ)

The module deals with quantifying the cyber-risk viz-a-viz expected loss calculation in the MMOG industry. The expected loss indicates the severity of the DDoS attack in terms of monetary loss to the firm. According to a Neustar report, a firm loses US$ 0.5 million per hour of a DDoS attack (Bezsonoff 2017; Sharma and Mukhopadhyay 2020b, 2020a; Tripathi and Mukhopadhyay 2020). We use this information to calculate loss and subsequently expected loss ($E(L)$), the product of the probability of attack with the loss incurred due to attack. (Campbell et al. 2003).

RQ2a: What is the expected loss ($E(L)$) from DDoS attacks on MMOG firms?

In the extant literature, expected loss values follow the long-tail distribution (Dutta and Perry 2011). Therefore,

RQ2b: What probability distribution best approximates the expected loss ($E(L)$) due to DDoS attacks on MMOG firms?

3.1.2.3. Cyber-risk Mitigation (CRM)

The final stage of the proposed model pertains to cyber-risk mitigation, suggesting ways to reduce the risk and the severity of the DDoS attacks in the MMOG industry. Risk (Probability of attack) values and severity (Expected loss) values serve as the primary inputs to this module. Our framework helps the MMOG firm CTO choose, based on Rational Choice Theory (Becker 1990; McCarthy 2002) and Protection-Motivation theory (Boss et al. 2015; Bulgurcu et al.

2010; Rogers 1975), between reducing (self-protection), accepting (self-insurance), or transferring (cyber-insurance) risk (Böhme 2005; Böhme and Schwartz 2006; Kesan et al. 2013; Majuca et al. 2006).

RQ3: What cyber-risk mitigation strategies should CTOs use for each kind of DDoS attack on MMOG platforms?

3.1.3. Cyber-risk management framework for online gaming firms: An Artificial Neural Network approach (FNN-CRAM)

According to the opportunity theory of crime, apart from the initial stimulus, the hacker looks out for vulnerabilities in the systems in an environment with minimal or no checks (or security controls) (Cohen and Felson 1979). Hackers also weigh their benefits compared to costs in terms of effort, time, and punishments, if any. On the other hand, firms under attack follow a layered approach towards fear appeals originating from cyber-attacks. They gauge the probability of the event's occurrence and the magnitude of its impact on them. Eventually, they enlist their protective responses and evaluate their efficacy (Boss et al. 2015; Bulgurcu et al. 2010; Rogers 1975). According to rational choice theory, decision-makers choose the alternative best suited to their subjective preference structure (Becker 1990; McCarthy 2002). The process of cyber-risk management closely follows from risk theory (Kunreuther 1997). It states that uncertain scenarios need to be dealt with risk assessment, quantification followed by mitigation by weighing costs and benefits. Based on the discussion above, our proposed FNN-CRAM model consists of three modules – Cyber-risk Assessment, Cyber-risk Quantification, and Cyber-mitigation for an MMOG firm, as shown in figure 3.5.

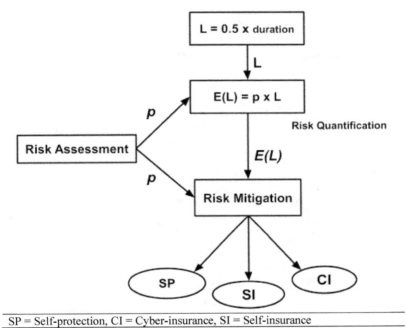

SP = Self-protection, CI = Cyber-insurance, SI = Self-insurance
Figure 3.5: FNN-CRAM model for MMOG firms

3.1.3.1. Cyber-risk Assessment (CRA)

We model each one of the five DDoS attacks separately to assess cyber-risk for an MMOG firm. We assume that DDoS attacks follow the binomial distribution, and their proportions in a particular quarter give the probability of their occurrence (Chen et al. 2011; McCullagh and Nelder 1989; Mukhopadhyay et al. 2019). Figure 3.6 depicts the cyber-risk assessment module.

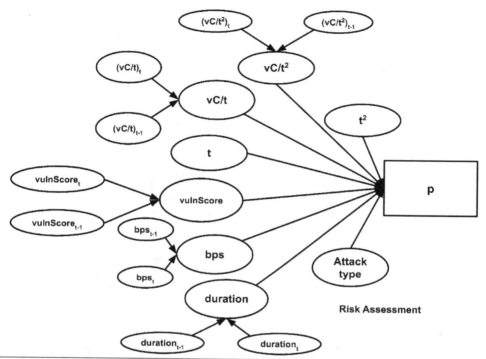

vC = Vulnerability count, t = Time, SP = Self-protection, CI = Cyber-insurance, SI = Self-insurance, Attack type = DNSFlood, NTPFlood, SSDPFlood, UC, UD

Figure 3.6: Cyber-risk assessment module for FNN-CRAM model

Table 3.2 provides literature support for the variables used in the proposed model.

Table 3.3: Model variables and relevant literature support

Variable name	Variable symbol	Literature
Attack type	Attack type	(McKeay 2017; Peng et al. 2007; Wang et al. 2020)
Attack intensity	bps_t, bps_{t-1}	(Peng et al. 2007; Tanenbaum and Wetherall 2010; Wang et al. 2020; Zhang et al. 2020)
Attack duration	$duration_t$, $duration_{t-1}$	(Peng et al. 2007; Tanenbaum and Wetherall 2010; Wang et al. 2020; Zhang et al. 2020)

Vulnerability Score	vulnScore$_t$, vulnScore$_{t-1}$	(Arora et al. 2008; Kannan and Telang 2005; Peng et al. 2007; Ransbotham et al. 2012; Shahriar and Zulkernine 2012; Zhang et al. 2020)
Vulnerability count	vC	(Arora et al. 2008; Kannan and Telang 2005; Peng et al. 2007; Ransbotham et al. 2012; Shahriar and Zulkernine 2012; Zhang et al. 2020)
Time	t, t^2	(Biswas and Mukhopadhyay 2018; Mukhopadhyay et al. 2019)
Vulnerability trend over t	$(vC/t)_t, (vC/t)_{t-1}$	(Cavusoglu et al. 2008, 2009; Ransbotham et al. 2012)
Vulnerability trend over t^2	$(vC/t^2)_t, (vC/t^2)_{t-1}$	Created for this study
Probability of attack for MMOG	p	(Biswas et al. 2017; Biswas and Mukhopadhyay 2018; Das et al. 2019; Mukhopadhyay et al. 2019)

As shown in figure 3.7, the probability (p_t) of DDoS attacks adversely slowing down the operations of an MMOG firm if the intensity of rogue traffic (bps) and its duration (duration) is high (Cavusoglu et al. 2008; Sharma and Mukhopadhyay 2020a; Yue et al. 2019).

	J	F	Mr	A	May	June	30th June	Jul	Ag	S	O	N	D
Days	0 to 180 days						225 days						
M	J	F	Mr	A	May	June	30th June	Jul	Ag	S	O	N	D
Q	Q1	Q1	Q1	Q2	Q2	Q2	Q2	Q3	Q3	Q3	Q4	Q4	Q4
TP	t-1			t				t+1			t+2		
SH							Jan	Feb	Mar	Apr	May	Jun	Jul
CERT	CERT: Vulnerability Q1 and Q2: Not disclosed						Vulnerability Q1 and Q2: Disclosed in a *lagged* manner						
MITRE	MITRE: CVSS for Q1 and Q2: Not disclosed						CVSS for vulnerabilities of Q1 and Q2 disclosed in a *lagged* manner						
H	Zero-Day attack by hackers												
OEM							*Patch creation*	*Patch release*					
								Patch deployment					
Firm	bps, duration = (High, High) for Q1 and Q2							bps, duration = (Low, Low)					
	p_t is high						p_t is high	p_{t+1} tends to reduce					

M= Months, Q = Quarters, TP =Time period, SH = Stakeholder, H = Hackers, OEM = Original Equipment Manufacturer

Figure 3.7: Stakeholder view of DDoS attack lifecycle

The probability (p_t) of a DDoS attack increases over time (t) as hackers repeatedly launch attacks by exploiting zero-day vulnerabilities in software used by MMOG firms (Mukhopadhyay et al. 2019; Wang et al. 2020). Computer emergency response team (CERT) takes six months (or two quarters) to disclose a vulnerability (Ransbotham et al. 2012) publicly. For example, on 30th June 2021 (where $t_{quarter} = 2$), the vulnerabilities from January to March 2021 ($t_{quarter} = 1$) and April to June 2021 ($t_{quarter} = 2$) are not yet disclosed by CERT. So, hackers can launch zero-day DDoS attacks by exploiting vulnerabilities (vC) from January to March 2021 and April to June 2021. Suppose CERT announces the vulnerabilities at the end of quarter 2 (i.e., 30th June 2021). Thus, on the 30th June 2021 ($t_{quarter} = 2$) and beyond, the overall vulnerabilities (vC/t) will come down as the technology vendors issue the respective patches. Moreover, the MMOG firms will increase security defenses (e.g., firewalls, cyber-insurance), train staff in best practices, design mitigation plans, and develop frameworks for bug-free software products (Angst et al. 2017; Cavusoglu et al. 2008). Thus, we suggest that vulnerabilities (vC/t and vC/t^2) tend to decrease over time which helps in reducing the probability (p_t) of DDoS attacks as security patches are available. By the end of June 2021 ($t_{quarter} = 2$), the hacker can exploit the vulnerabilities of quarters 1 and 2, respectively. Thus we intend to model the probability of DDoS attack (p_t) using lagged variables such as $(vC/t)_t$, $(vC/t^2)_{t-1}$, as this phenomenon can be equated to autoregressive model (Geurts et al. 1977; Gujarati 2009). Similarly, the hacker tends to launch a high-intensity and longer duration zero-day DDoS attack because of the unavailability of security patches in quarters 1 and 2 (i.e., Jan to March and April to June 2021). Thus, we intend to model the DDoS attack (p_t) probability using lagged variables such as bps_{t-1} and $duration_{t-1}$ (Geurts et al. 1977; Gujarati 2009).

Similarly, in August 2021, NIST and MITRE publicly announce the vulnerabilities' details along with the severity score (i.e., CVSS). As a result, the technology vendors focus on creating security patches for vulnerabilities with the highest severity scores (i.e., vscr) (Arora et al. 2008; Kannan and Telang 2005). It will reduce the probability (p_t) of DDoS attacks. They have higher chances of culminating in attacks because they take longer to get patched before being exploited (Biswas et al. 2016; Cavusoglu et al. 2008; Das et al. 2019; Peng et al. 2007; Tripathi and Mukhopadhyay 2020).

Thus, we investigate

RQ1a: What is the proportion (probability) of each kind of DDoS attack compromising the MMOG systems?

Our model estimates the probability ($0<p<1$) that a DDoS attack occurs to assess the cyber-risk for each kind of DDoS attack. The first stage of this model helps us estimate the probability for each type of DDoS attack by training, validating, and testing the Feedforward Neural Network (FNN) (Hagan and Demuth 2014). The extant literature has used Weibull distribution to model the probability of failures. Thus, we also test whether the probability of a DDoS attack follows the same.

RQ 1b: Which probability distribution best approximates the occurrence of DDoS attacks in the MMOG industry?

3.1.3.2. Cyber-risk Quantification (CRQ)

The next stage of the proposed model deals with quantifying the cyber-risk viz-a-viz expected loss calculation. DDoS attack results in disruption of service to legitimate users. Thus, the loss due to DDoS attack is proportional to the duration of the attack (Bezsonoff 2017; Yue et al. 2019). The expected loss indicates the severity of the DDoS attack in terms of monetary loss to the firm. According to a Neustar report, a firm loses US$ 0.5 million per hour of a DDoS attack (Bezsonoff 2017; Sharma and Mukhopadhyay 2020b, 2020a; Tripathi and Mukhopadhyay

2020). We use this information to calculate loss and subsequently expected loss (Courtney 1977), the product of the probability of attack with the loss incurred due to attack (Campbell et al. 2003). In the extant literature, expected loss values follow the long-tail distribution, and thus, we check if gamma distribution best approximates the same (Dutta and Perry 2011).

RQ2a: What is the expected loss for each type of DDoS attack in the MMOG industry?

RQ 2b: What probability distribution best estimates the expected loss caused due to each type of DDoS attack in the MMOG industry?

3.1.3.3. Cyber-risk Mitigation (CRM)

The final stage of the proposed model pertains to cyber-risk mitigation by suggesting ways to reduce the risk and the severity of the DDoS attacks in the MMOG industry. The primary inputs for this stage are the risk (Probability of attack) values and severity (Expected loss) values. These help us decide whether the firm CTO should choose between reducing (self-protection), accepting (self-insurance), or transferring (cyber-insurance) risk (Böhme 2005; Böhme and Schwartz 2006; Kesan et al. 2013, 2005; Majuca et al. 2006).

RQ3: What cyber-risk mitigation strategies should CTOs use for each kind of DDoS attack in MMOG firms?

3.1.4. Text mining-based cyber-risk assessment for DDoS attacks and mitigation using cyber-insurance (TCRAM)

As shown in Figure 3.8, our proposed model follow from the risk theory (Kunreuther, 1997) that uncertain scenarios require resolution in three interdependent steps, our proposed model consists of three modules: cyber risk assessment (CRA), cyber risk quantification (CRQ), and cyber risk mitigation (CRM). The model takes the news articles from the Internet and outputs possible risk mitigation strategies by estimating the probability of detecting the DDoS attack traits correctly and the subsequent expected loss in intermediate steps.

3.1.4.1. Cyber-risk Assessment (CRA)

In the event of a DDOS attack, a firm tends to lose revenue as well as reputation due to the loss of productive hours. Thus, the CTO is evaluating the business environment for threats such as hackers to reduce losses for the firm. In order to evaluate the threats, they need to infer the likelihood as well as the severity of these attacks. It is in line with the threat appraisal in terms of likelihood as well as severity (Boss *et al.*, 2015; Rogers, 1975).

According to PMT theory, to minimize the propensity of DDoS attacks, CTOs would tend to spend a substantial amount of their IT budget on perimeter security solutions to reduce the probability of DDoS attacks (D'Arcy *et al.*, 2020; Dhillon and Backhouse, 2000), which is in concurrence with a threat appraisal. Security solutions and spending are essential points for a firm to defend against potential DDoS attacks proactively. It also suggests that in the event of a DDoS attack, top management plays an integral part in allaying the fears of the firm's customers and employees. We also observe that customer confidence and trust are crucial when assessing risk due to DDoS attacks. CTO can gather information about these attacks from public forums reporting attack features such as attack size, cost. Cybersecurity analysts report

DDoS attack-specific information on these forums after carefully analyzing the multiple sources. In the event of an imminent attack, they can take proactive mitigation steps to counter or reduce the impact of the attacks. If the CTO misinterprets the threats or ignores them, the firms incur losses due to the delay. Thus, it becomes critical to reduce the likelihood of misinterpretation of information from these forums and reduce the severity of these attacks by either timely mitigation or cyber-insurance policies.

Table 3.4: Relevant inputs and their literature support

Inputs	Literature support
Text tokens	Han, Kamber and Pei 2017; Li et al. 2018
Topics related to security	Wang et al. 2013a; Yue et al. 2019; Wang et al. 2013b
Cyber-risk quantification themes	Dutta and Perry 2011
Cyber-risk mitigation themes	Cavusoglu et al. 2008; Rejda 2013; Kesan et al. 2005; 2013

Figure 3.8 depicts the proposed model for the aforesaid.

RQ 1(a): What are the attack traits of DDoS attacks evident determined from web articles?

RQ 1(b): What is the probability of getting attacked by a hacker if the decision-maker misinterprets the DDoS attack traits?

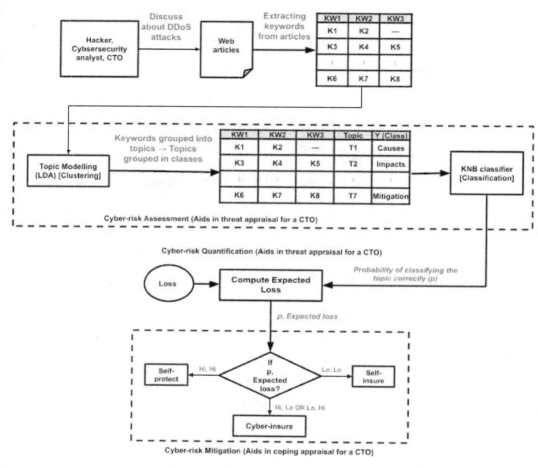

Figure 3.8: Flowchart of the proposed TCRAM model

3.1.4.2. Cyber-risk Quantification (CRQ)

If the CTO misinterprets the threats or ignores them, the firms incur losses due to the delay. Thus, it becomes critical to reduce the likelihood of misinterpretation of information from these forums and reduce the severity of these attacks by either timely mitigation or cyber-insurance policies (Kunreuther 1997b). We devise these strategies (response efficacy) and decide upon them according to the CTO subjective preference structure (self-efficacy) and cost associated with each such strategy (Herath and Rao, 2009).

RQ 2: What is the distribution which best estimates the impact of the DDoS attack on customers?

3.1.4.3. Cyber-risk Mitigation (CRM)

Thereafter, they need to devise mitigation strategies in order to reduce both the risk and severity of DDOS attacks. It follows from the coping appraisal estimation of PMT. According to Rational choice theory (Becker, 1990; McCarthy, 2002), a decision-maker weighs the costs and benefits of diverse choices, choosing the option most closely aligned with their subjective preference structure, which concurs with a coping appraisal. Thus, it becomes critical to reduce the likelihood of misinterpretation of information from these forums and reduce the severity of these attacks by either timely mitigation or cyber-insurance policies. We devise these strategies (response efficacy) and decide upon them according to the CTO subjective preference structure (self-efficacy) and cost associated with each such strategy (Herath and Rao, 2009). They consider the firm's risk profile and decide which are the appropriate technological and financial interventions to reduce (self-protection), accept (self-insurance), or transfer (cyber-insurance) risk (Böhme, 2005; Böhme and Schwartz, 2006; Kesan *et al.*, 2013; Majuca *et al.*, 2006).

RQ 3: What mitigation strategies should be used for these DDoS attacks?

3.2. Smart Cities

Unlike the earlier digital ecosystem, smart cities usually suffer from availability as well as data integrity issues. Malicious actors can disrupt the normal workflow of smart cities by tampering with different smart systems and their sensors. In the subsequent studies, we focus on integrated traffic management systems in smart cities. The speed of vehicles is an important indicator of optimal functioning of the smart city pathways, and thus any tampering with its value through sensors leads to congestion or collision on roads. We design two studies for the aforesaid to model tampering of speed-sensing sensors residing on autonomous vehicles and sensors residing outside the vehicles (i.e., street intersections). First, we propose a SARIMA-based cyber-risk assessment and mitigation framework (SCRAM) to address tampering of sensors residing outside the vehicles. On the other hand, the second study proposes a deep learning-based cyber-risk assessment and mitigation framework (DL-CRAM) to address the tampering of speed sensors residing on the vehicles. Figure 3.9 illustrates the aforesaid with both cyber-risk management frameworks.

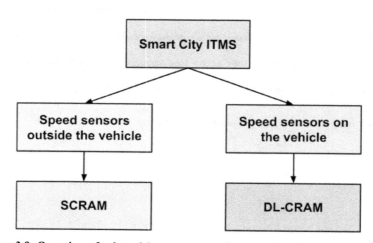

Figure 3.9: Overview of cyber-risk management frameworks related to smart cities

3.2.1. SARIMA-based cyber-risk assessment and mitigation model for a smart city's traffic management systems (SCRAM)

As shown in Figure 3.10, our proposed SCRAM model was developed based on protection motivation theory (PMT) (Boss et al. 2015; Kleindorfer and Kunreuther 1999; Rogers 1975). The model incorporates threat appraisal (Boss et al. 2015; Herath and Rao 2009; Rogers 1975) regarding the probability of speed anomalies (Kim et al. 2021) and subsequently estimates the severity of such errors as monetary losses. We devise our mitigation strategies using these metrics, which form an essential part of the coping appraisal. We devise these strategies (response efficacy) and decide upon them according to the city administrator's subjective preference structure (self-efficacy) and cost associated with each such strategy (Boss et al. 2015; Herath and Rao 2009; Rogers 1975). The model takes the average speed as read by sensors from the integrated traffic management system and outputs possible risk mitigation strategies by estimating the probability of encountering anomalous speed and the subsequent expected loss in intermediate steps.

3.2.1.1. Cyber-risk Assessment (CRA)

In line with the threat appraisal component of protection-motivation theory (Cheng et al. 2020; Neumann et al. 2019), the CRA module takes the average speed time-series data as input and feeds them to a forecasting module. This model learns the speed patterns over time and aims to correctly classify the unseen speed sample in a particular observational window (Böhme and Kataria 2006; Herath and Rao 2009; Hoffman et al. 1978). Thus, calculating the number of anomalous records out of total speed reading for each month (Baskerville 1993; Herath and Rao 2009; Mukhopadhyay et al. 2007; Ozier 1989; Rogers 1975), we estimate the probability that citizens would encounter anomalous speeds through ITMS. Based on Risk theory, these probabilities will aid the city administrator in identifying three distinct classes of risk arising from hacker-induced speed distortions (Guarro 1987). Table 3.5 details the variables used in this study and relevant literature support.

Table 3.5: Relevant variables and their literature support

Variables	Literature support
Average speed	Cheng, Pang, Pavlou 2020; Xu et al. 2019
Sensor data	Hiller and Blanke, 2017; yue et al. 2019

Thus, we investigate the foolwing:

RQ1(a): What is the probability of predicting the average speed of a vehicle correctly when the hacker has tampered with the ITMS?

RQ1(b): What distribution best approximates the probability of predicting the average speed of a vehicle correctly when the hacker has tampered with the ITMS?

Figure 3.10 illustrates the proposed model for the aforesaid.

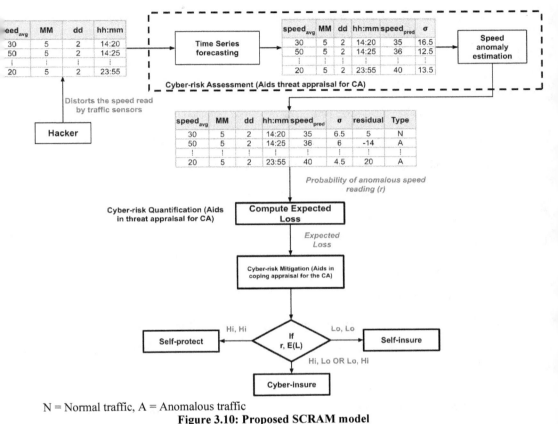

N = Normal traffic, A = Anomalous traffic

Figure 3.10: Proposed SCRAM model

3.2.1.2. Cyber-risk Quantification (CRQ)

The CRQ module estimates the expected loss due to each speed anomaly by using actual and misread speed difference. The difference is directly proportional to the loss. Thus, based on risk theory, the probability of misreading is multiplied by the loss to compute the expected monetary loss (Bulgurcu et al. 2010; Herath and Rao 2009). Thus, it follows,

RQ2(a): What is the impact of wrongly predicting the average speed of a vehicle when the hacker has tampered with the ITMS?

RQ 2(b): What distribution best approximates the expected loss due to wrongly predicting the vehicle's average speed when the hacker has tampered with the ITMS?

3.2.1.3. Cyber-risk Mitigation (CRM)

The proposed model's final stage pertains to cyber risk mitigation; in this stage, we suggest ways to reduce the risk and severity of speed anomalies due to cyberattacks in smart cities. The module's primary inputs are the risk values (probability of an attack) and severity values (expected loss). According to rational choice theory (Kahneman and Tversky 1979; McCarthy 2002), a decision-maker weighs the costs and benefits of diverse choices, choosing whichever option is closely aligned with their subjective preference structure. Similarly, smart-city administrators are concerned with reducing risk and severity; thus, modeling the utility of both of these choices becomes necessary. Finally, they consider the smart city's risk profile and decide which are the appropriate technological and financial interventions to reduce (self-protection), accept (self-insurance), or transfer (cyber-insurance) risk (Böhme and Kataria 2006; Kesan et al. 2013; Majuca et al. 2006; Rejda 2007). Thus, we investigate:

RQ3: What ways to mitigate incorrect average speed predictions when the hacker has tampered with the ITMS?

3.2.2. Cyber-risk Assessment and Mitigation framework for smart cities: A deep learning approach (DL-CRAM)

Our proposed DL-CRAM model, as shown in Figure 3.11, was developed based on protection motivation theory (PMT) (Boss et al. 2015; Kleindorfer and Kunreuther 1999; Rogers 1975). The model incorporates threat appraisal (Boss et al. 2015; Herath and Rao 2009; Rogers 1975) regarding the probability of misreading two-digit speed limit (i.e., 00 to 99) signs tampered with by hackers (Kim et al. 2021) and subsequently estimates the severity of such errors as monetary losses. We devise our mitigation strategies using these metrics, which form an essential part of the coping appraisal. We devise these strategies (response efficacy) and decide upon them according to the city administrator's subjective preference structure (self-efficacy) and cost associated with each such strategy (Boss et al. 2015; Herath and Rao 2009; Rogers 1975). The model takes the speed limit from the integrated traffic management system and outputs possible risk mitigation strategies by estimating the probability of detecting the speed correctly and the subsequent expected loss in intermediate steps.

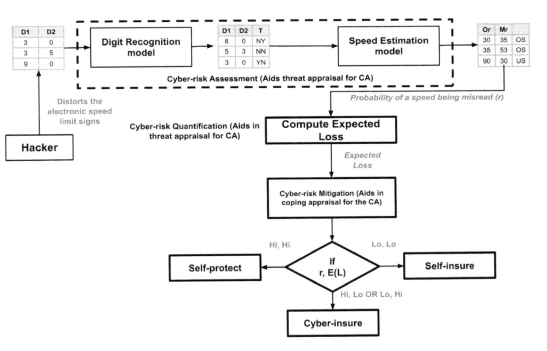

Figure 3.11: Proposed DL-CRAM model

Table 3.6 details the variables used in this study along with relevant literature support.

Table 3.6: Relevant variables and their literature support

Variables	Literature support
Average speed	Cheng, Pang, Pavlou 2020; Xu et al. 2019
Sensor data	Hiller and Blanke, 2017; yue et al. 2019

3.2.2.1. Cyber Risk Assessment (CRA)

In line with the threat appraisal component of protection-motivation theory (Herath and Rao 2009; Rogers 1975), the CRA module takes the speed limit sign images as input and feeds them to a digit recognition model. This model learns the speed limits and aims to correctly classify the unseen sample of two-digit speed limits (Mukhopadhyay et al. 2013; Sharma and Mukhopadhyay 2020c, 2020b). Table 3.7 shows that the autonomous vehicle might misread the two-digit speed limit under three different scenarios despite using a digit recognition model. Thus, using Bayesian inference (Das et al. 2019; Han et al. 2017; Hastie et al. 2009; I. B. Hossack et al. 1999; Sharma and Mukhopadhyay 2020c), we study the following : (i) only the first digit (D1) is incorrectly read (NY scenario) with the conditional probability (r) of q_1*p_3, (ii) only the second digit (D2) is incorrectly read (YN scenario) with the conditional probability (r) of p_1*q_2, and (iii) both digits are incorrectly read (e.g., NN scenario) with the conditional probability of q_1*q_3. Based on Risk theory, these conditional probabilities will aid the city administrator in identifying three distinct classes of risk arising from hacker-induced speed limit distortions (Kunreuther 1997b).

Table 3.7: Impact of misreading speeds

D1	D2	Original Speed	Misread Speed	r
N	Y	30	80	q1 * p3
Y	N	90	30	p1 * q2
N	N	35	53	q1 * q3

Thus, it follows,

RQ 1(a): What is the probability of misreading only the first, second, or both in a two-digit speed limit sign?

Next, we aim to estimate the probability distribution of the risk due to misreading speed limit signs to best approximate the risk probability (Bezsonoff 2017). Thus, it follows

RQ1(b): What distribution best approximates the probability of misreading the two-digit speed limit sign?

3.2.2.2. Cyber Risk Quantification (CRQ)

The CRQ module estimates the expected loss due to each speed misreading by computing it using the difference in actual and misread speed. The difference is directly proportional to the loss. Thus, based on risk theory, the probability of misreading is multiplied by the loss to compute the expected monetary loss (Campbell et al. 2003; Dutta and Perry 2011; Sharma and Mukhopadhyay 2020c; Tripathi and Mukhopadhyay 2020). Thus, it follows

RQ 2(a): What is the impact of misreading only the first, second, or both in a two-digit speed limit sign?

Next, we infer the probability distribution for the expected loss for the above three scenarios. Extant literature suggests that loss amounts follow a long-tail distribution where small losses are frequent while large loss amounts are rare (Becker 1978). Thus, we investigate

RQ 2(b): What distribution best approximates the expected loss due to misclassifying speeds?

3.2.2.3. Cyber Risk Mitigation (CRM)

The proposed model's final stage pertains to cyber risk mitigation; in this stage, we suggest ways to reduce the risk and severity of speed misreading due to cyberattacks in smart cities. The module's primary inputs are the risk values (probability of an attack) and severity values (expected loss). According to rational choice theory (Böhme 2005; McCarthy 2002), a decision-maker weighs the costs and benefits of diverse choices, choosing whichever option is closely aligned with their subjective preference structure. Similarly, smart-city administrators are concerned with reducing risk and severity; thus, modeling the utility of both of these choices becomes necessary. Finally, they consider the smart city's risk profile and decide which are the appropriate technological and financial interventions to reduce (self-protection), accept (self-insurance), or transfer (cyber-insurance) risk (Böhme and Schwartz 2006; Bulgurcu et al. 2010; Han et al. 2017; Kesan et al. 2013; Mukhopadhyay et al. 2013). Thus, we investigate:

RQ 3: What are ways to mitigate cyber risk due to misreading only the first, second, or both in a two-digit speed limit sign?

3.3. Crowdfunding platforms

Crowdfunding platforms present a unique set of challenges in eliminating fraud campaigns. Fraud campaigns are detrimental for the platform, resulting in losing platform fees and damaging its integrity amongst campaign creators and funder alike. The process of cyber-risk management provides us with a tool to quantify the aforesaid cyber-risk in terms of likelihood and severity, thereby indicating the scale of this problem for crowdfunding firms. Our framework closely follows from risk theory (Kunreuther 1997a). It states that uncertain scenarios need to be dealt with risk assessment, quantification followed by mitigation by weighing costs and benefits. Based on the discussion above, our proposed BCRAM model consists of three modules – Cyber-risk Assessment, Cyber-risk Quantification, and Cyber-mitigation for an MMOG firm, as shown in figure 3.12.

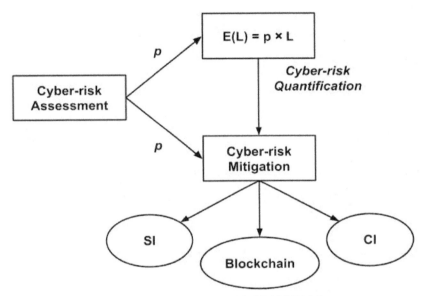

Figure 3.12: Proposed BCRAM model

3.3.1. Cyber-risk Assessment (CRA)

Figure 3.12 illustrates that crowdfunding campaigns' success can be attributed to two types of traits. First, the campaign-specific traits are visible on the platform and serve as a stimulus for the funders to donate funds to a particular campaign. Campaign-specific traits include the goal amount of the campaign, the total amount pledged, the number of backers supporting it, the length of the campaign title, and the amount pledged by each backer. These traits inform funders about the credibility and viability of the campaign (Burtch et al. 2013).

Figure 3.13: Diagram for Cyber-risk Assessment module

Creator traits aim to capture external and platform-specific network effects and how this affects the success of a campaign. These traits have two components, namely — platform-specific and social media-specific. The platform-specific traits include the number of campaigns backed and created by the founder. On the other hand, social media-specific traits include the follower and friend count of the founder. We intend to investigate the following research questions as an exploratory empirical study of the crowdfunding platform Kickstarter. Table 3.8 details relevant literature support for the variables used in this study.

Table 3.8: Relevant variables and their literature support

Variables	Literature Support
pledged_amount	Burtch et al. 2013; Andreoni 1995; Bardsley and Sausgruber 2005; Chauduri and Paichayontvijit 2006; Croson and Shang 2008; Shang and Croson 2009
goal_amount	Burtch et al. 2013; Andreoni 1995; Bardsley and Sausgruber 2005; Chauduri and Paichayontvijit 2006; Croson and Shang 2008; Shang and Croson 2009
num_of_backers	Burtch et al. 2013; Schwienbacher and Larralde 2010; Belleflamme et al. 2014
backer_ratio	Burtch et al. 2013; Schwienbacher and Larralde 2010; Belleflamme et al. 2014
num_of_backed	Burtch et al. 2013; Wessel et al. 2014
num_of_created	Burtch et al. 2013; Wessel et al. 2014
friend_count	Burtch et al. 2013; Wessel et al. 2014; Hong et al. 2018
follower_count	Burtch et al. 2013; Wessel et al. 2014; Hong et al. 2018

Thus, we investigate:

RQ1: What is the probability that a crowdfunding campaign will fail?

3.3.2. Cyber-risk Quantification (CRQ)

The module quantifies the cyber-risk viz-a-viz expected loss calculation for crowdfunding platforms. The expected loss indicates the monetary loss to the firm due to the onboarding of fraudulent campaigns. A crowdfunding platform loses 5% of the goal amount (i.e., platform fee) (Aldrich 2014). We use this information to calculate loss and subsequently expected loss (E(L)), the product of the probability of attack with the loss incurred due to attack (Campbell et al. 2003).

RQ2: What is the expected loss when a campaign fails?

3.3.3. Cyber-risk Mitigation (CRM)

The final stage of the proposed model pertains to cyber-risk mitigation, suggesting ways to reduce the risk and the severity of the campaign misclassification on crowdfunding platforms. Risk (Probability of attack) values and severity (Expected loss) values serve as the primary inputs to this module. Our framework helps the platform's CTO choose, based on Rational Choice Theory (Becker 1990; McCarthy 2002) and Protection-Motivation theory (Boss et al. 2015; Bulgurcu et al. 2010; Rogers 1975), between reducing (self-protection), accepting (self-insurance), or transferring (cyber-insurance) risk (Böhme 2005; Böhme and Schwartz 2006; Kesan et al. 2013; Majuca et al. 2006).

RQ3: What are the ways to mitigate risk due to misclassification of campaign success?

4. Methodology

This section details the methodology employed across different studies across three digital ecosystems being studied — MMOG platforms, smart cities, and crowdfunding platforms. We have used a mix of data mining, econometric, and simulation methods to answer each studies' research questions.

4.1. Massively Multiplayer Online Gaming (MMOG) platforms

We analyze DDoS attacks on MMOG platforms in different steps according to various predictors, namely, attack traits and vulnerability data. We propose four studies in conjunction with this to predict the probability of DDoS attacks on MMOG platforms. We use the Kernel naïve Bayes classifier, logit and probit models, and feedforward neural networks to quantify the risk values for DDoS attacks. Subsequently, in the quantification module, we calculate expected loss as the product of loss due to DDoS attacks with the probability of such breaches. We undertake the following studies, namely, KB-CRAM, CRAMOG, FNN-CRAM, and TCRAM. The first three studies use structured data like attack attributes and vulnerability data. In contrast, the fourth study uses unstructured data such as text from web articles. Figure 4.1 depicts the different studies related to MMOG platforms.

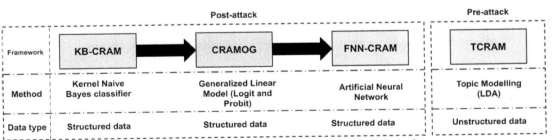

Figure 4.1: Overview of methodologies used for MMOG platforms

4.1.1. Kernel naïve Bayes classifier-based cyber-risk assessment and mitigation framework for online gaming platforms (KB-CRAM)

This section describes the methods used in each module of the KB-CRAM framework. We have used only attack intensity and duration for this posthoc analysis. Firms can only gather attack traits immediately after cyberattacks. Thus, it gives them a credible estimate of the lower end of the attack probability and severity for deciding investment strategies.

4.1.1.1. Cyber-risk Assessment (CRA)

We used two data mining methods in conjunction with the CRA module, namely, supervised (classification) and unsupervised (clustering) learning methods, to identify DDoS attacks in the MMOG industry, as described later. In supervised learning modules, the dataset contained the target class label, and thus, algorithms aimed to learn patterns amongst predictors to map them to particular class labels. Conversely, an unsupervised learning module aims to group similar-looking data records into undefined classes using distance measures (Han et al. 2012).

We used a kernel naïve Bayes (KNB) classification method to classify overlapping DDoS attacks. In this study, we chose the Naïve Bayes classifier as the DDoS attacks' features (i.e., attack intensity and attack duration) are independent of each other (Han, Kamber, and Pei 2017; Silverman 2018). The attack features did not follow any known distribution. Therefore, we chose the Kernel naïve Bayes classifier, which uses the kernel density estimation method to estimate the continuous variables' probability density function (pdf) (Hastie, Tibshirani, and Friedman 2009). For this study, the classifier's accuracy informs us about the probability of detecting a DDoS attack correctly (Han, Kamber, and Pei 2017). Thus, according to the initial accuracy and confusion matrix, we chose the class with the highest misclassifications to split into finer classes to boost the classifier's accuracy (Han, Kamber, and Pei 2017).

Next, our CRA module generated a dendrogram for the DDoS attack class with the highest misclassification rate to decide the clusters' ideal number to split it (Han, Kamber, and Pei 2017). Next, we split this class into an optimal number (output from the dendrogram) of clusters using the k-means clustering algorithm with bps and duration as DDoS attack features. We observed that the classifier's accuracy increased with every subsequent split of overlapping classes (Hastie, Tibshirani, and Friedman 2009). Our iterative CRA module stopped once the classifier did not incrementally change the overall model accuracy due to class splitting. Otherwise, we halted it once the model accuracy crossed a threshold τ (chosen as at least 90% in this study). The threshold τ was selected depending on the criticality of the online mode of operation vis-à-vis overall operations.

4.1.1.2. Cyber-risk Quantification (CRQ)

We computed the expected loss at a rate of US$ 0.5 million per hour during the DDoS attack, as shown in equation 2 (Courtney 1977; Bezsonoff 2017).

4.1.1.3. Cyber-risk Mitigation (CRM)

Our model suggests ways to accept, transfer, or reduce cyber-risk using technological and financial tools (Rejda 2007; Böhme and Schwartz 2006; Böhme and Kataria 2006).

Table 4.1 describes the methodology used to assess cyber-risk and suggest subsequent mitigation strategies.

Table 4.1: Steps in the KB-CRAM model

Step	
Step 1	Pass training dataset (TD) to KNB classifier
	Cyber-risk Assessment (CRA):
Step 2	KNB classifier assigns all records to classes based on the dominant posterior probability
Step 3	Calculate accuracy (p) of detecting DDoS attack by the classifier: $p = KNB\ (bps,\ duration,\ AT_1,\ AT_2...,\ AT_7)$ **(Supervised Learning – Classification)**
Step 4	If accuracy (p) < threshold τ,
Step 5	Select class with minimum p
Step 6	Generate dendrogram for this class and the optimal number of clusters 'k.'
Step 7	Split into 'k' sub-classes using the *k-means algorithm* **(Unsupervised learning – Clustering)**
Step 8	Go to *step 2*
Step 9	Else go to Step 10
Step 10	**Cyber-risk Quantification (CRQ)** Expected loss, $E(L) = (1-p) * (0.5 * duration)$ **Cyber-risk Mitigation (CRM)** **Propose Risk Mitigation strategies (technology, cyber insurance)**
Step 11	*If (1-p) > 0.5 AND E(L) > 7 million, then implement Self-protection (SP)* *Else if (1-p) < 0.5 AND E(L) < 7 million then implement Cyber-insurance (CI)* *Else subscribe to Self-insurance (SI)*

4.1.2. A logit-based Cyber-risk Assessment and Mitigation model for Massively Multiplayer Online Gaming (CRAMOG) platforms

This section describes the methods used in each module of the CRAMOG framework. Unlike the previous section, this study uses attack traits and vulnerability data to increase the predictive accuracy of the model. It also factors the time component, which is crucial as the probability of attacks can differ over time depending upon interventions used by the firm or increase hackers' competency.

4.1.2.1. Cyber-risk Assessment (CRA)

We use the Generalized Linear Model (GLM) (i.e., logit and probit models) (McCullagh and Nelder 1989) to predict the probability of 5 five types of DDoS attacks in each quarter. We have validated our logit (M1) and probit (M2) models using the chi-square goodness-of-fit test (McCullagh and Nelder 1989). We use a beta distribution to approximate the risk due to DDoS attacks, as shown in equation 3 (Hossack et al. 1983; Mukhopadhyay et al. 2019).

4.1.2.2. Cyber-risk Quantification (CRQ)

Next, we assume that firms lose US$ 0.5 million loss per hour of the DDoS attack. Subsequently, we compute the expected loss for each data record, and a gamma distribution is fitted to the same, as shown in equation 4 (Dutta and Perry 2011; Mukhopadhyay et al. 2019).

4.1.2.3. Cyber-risk Mitigation (CRM)

Subsequently, we suggest mitigation strategies by appropriately visualizing the risk (probability of the attack) and severity (expected loss of the attack). We use a 2×2 heat matrix to help the firm choose between self-protection, self-insurance, or cyber-insurance depending upon the boundary values for high-low risk and severity values.

4.1.3. Cyber-risk management framework for online gaming firms: An Artificial Neural Network approach (FNN-CRAM)

This section details the methods used in the FNN-CRAM framework. Similar to the previous section, we use attack traits and vulnerability data. We use data from both current and prior quarters to increase the predictive accuracy. The research methodology consists of three prominent stages: cyber-risk assessment, cyber-risk quantification, and cyber-risk Mitigation.

4.1.3.1. Cyber-risk Assessment (CRA)

In the cyber-risk assessment stage, we identify the assets that increase the vulnerability of information systems to DDoS attacks. The second stage quantifies the cyber-risk of DDoS attacks with the help of variables mentioned earlier. We use the probability and severity of attacks in the last step to suggest mitigation strategies to absorb the cyber-risk.

$p_t = FNN(bps_t, bps_{t-1}, dur_t, dur_{t-1}, t, t^2, (vc/t)_t, (vc/t^2)_t, (vc/t)_{t-1}, (vc/t^2)_{t-1}, vscr_t, vscr_{t-1})$

We propose a feedforward neural network (FNN) to compute the probability (p_t) of five kinds of DDoS attacks on an MMOG firm. The probability (p_t) of attack depends on time-dependent variables such as bps, duration, vulnerability score, and counts. We use these variables from both the current quarter (t) as well as the previous quarter (t-1) as discussed in the proposed model (Geurts et al. 1977; Gujarati 2009). FNN has been used extensively to model time-series data and performs better for independent variables with non-linearity (Allende et al. 2002; Desai and Bharati 1998; Krohn et al. 2019). Thus, we have chosen an FNN over classification techniques such as Decision trees, SVM, K-nearest neighbor method, and logistic regression (Han et al. 2017). Our proposed FNN model consists of three layers, namely, the input (I) layer, the hidden (H) layer, and the output (O) layer. FNN topology consists of seven input neurons, ten hidden neurons, and one output neuron (Hagan and Demuth 2014). Our FNN model takes the input in the form of the independent variables (i.e., bps, duration, vC/t, vC/t², vscr), which are non-linear with respect to the dependent variable (p_t). Each neuron in the FNN behaves like a multi-input regression model (Hagan and Demuth 2014; Kelleher and Tierney 2018). Inputs are multiplied by weights generated through the Nguyen-Widrow algorithm (Nguyen and Widrow 1990). Next, the product passes through a transfer function such as log-sigmoid, which adjusts for the non-linearity in the inputs. Finally, the probability (p_t) of attacks, which lies between zero to one, is computed through the satlins transfer function.

We use an 80:10:10 ratio for training, validation, and testing datasets (Hagan and Demuth 2014; Han et al. 2017). The Levenberg-Marquardt algorithm trains the FNN until meeting the stopping criterion (i.e., either minimum gradient or validation stop) (Levenberg 1944). We use Mean Squared Error (MSE) as the metric to evaluate the training, validation, and testing performance (Hagan and Demuth 2014). The trained FNN computes the probability (or proportion) of each kind of DDoS attack. Next, we fit a Weibull distribution to the computed probabilities (or proportions) and estimate its parameter (I. B. Hossack et al. 1999). Using the estimated parameters, we calculate the mean and standard deviation for each kind of DDoS attack.

4.1.3.2. Cyber-risk Quantification (CRQ)

On the other hand, the loss in each DDoS attack is calculated using a US$ 0.5 million loss per hour (Bezsonoff 2017). Expected Loss for each data record is computed and a gamma distribution fitted to the same (Dutta and Perry 2011). Mean and standard deviation values for expected loss for each DDoS attack follow.

4.1.3.3. Cyber-risk Mitigation (CRM)

The next stage of the study suggests mitigation strategies by appropriately visualizing the risk (probability of the attack) and severity (expected loss of the attack). We use a 2×2 heat matrix to help the firm choose between self-protection, self-insurance, or cyber-insurance depending upon the boundary values for high-low risk and severity values (Mukhopadhyay et al. 2019). The firms should choose self-protection if they have high risk-high severity attacks (Rejda 2007). Firms with low risk-high severity (or vice-versa) attacks should go for cyber-insurance (Majuca et al. 2006). Low risk-Low severity attacks on firms should be self-insured to absorb the losses (Kesan et al. 2005). Table 4.2 details the algorithm used for analyzing the DDoS attacks.

Table 4.2: Steps in the FNN-CRAM model

	Cyber-risk Assessment
Step 1	**Input:** $D = (Y_D, X_D)$ $Y_D = p$ $X_D = [bps_t, duration_t, t, t^2, vulnScore_t, (vC/t)_t, (vC/t^2)_t,$ # t quarter $bps_{t-1}, duration_{t-1}, vulnScore_{t-1}, (vC/t)_{t-1}, (vC/t^2)_{t-1}]$ # (t-1) quarter
Step 2	**Output:** $p_t = FNN(D_{training})$ # Topology 7-10-1 # Initialize the weights using the Nguyen-Widrow algorithm. # $D_{training} : D_{validation} : D_{testing} = 80:10:10$ If $MSE(p) = min\_threshold$ Then stop the training
Step 3	Fit Weibull distribution on *p* values
	Cyber-risk Quantification
Step 4	Expected loss, $E(L) = p * 0.5 * (duration)$
Step 5	Fit a Gamma distribution on *E(L)* values
	Cyber-risk mitigation

Step 6	Propose mitigation strategies *If p = Hi* AND *E(L) = Hi, then* Self-Protection (SP) *Else if p = Hi* AND *E(L) = Lo* OR *p = Lo* AND *E(L) = Hi, then* Self-insurance (SI) *Else if p = Lo* AND *E(L) = Lo, then* Cyber-insurance (CI)

FNN = Feedforward Neural Network

4.1.4. Text mining-based cyber-risk assessment for DDoS attacks and mitigation using cyber-insurance (TCRAM)

This section details the methodology used in TCRAM framework.

4.1.4.1. Cyber-risk Assessment (CRA)

In order to prepare the text corpus for topic modeling in subsequent sections, we filter unnecessary tokens by using a cut-off tf-idf score after pre-processing the data by following the undermentioned steps. Table 4.3 shows the steps involved in pre-processing the text corpus.

Table 4.3: Pre-processing steps for the text from web articles

Step 1	Scrape text data from web articles using python.
Step 2	Tokenize the text into words using periods, comma, etc., as separators.
Step 3	Add parts-of-speech (POS) to tokens.
Step 4	Add named-entity details to the tokens.
Step 5	Remove the common stopwords (such as prepositions, conjunctions, etc.)
Step 6	Normalize the tokens by lemmatizing them to POS-based root words.
Step 7	Calculate TF-IDF score for each token using: $tf(t,d)$ = count of t in d / number of words in d $idf(t) = \log_2(N/df(t)) = \log_2(N/N(t))$

tf-idf(t,d) = tf(t,d) * idf(t)

where,

df(t) = N(t)

df(t) = Document frequency of a term t

N(t) = Number of documents containing the term t

Step 8   Remove tokens with tf-idf(t,d) < τ

4.1.4.1.1. *Latent Dirichlet Allocation (Clustering)*

This module uses a hybrid approach comprising an unsupervised text mining method, such as Latent Dirichlet Allocation (LDA), and supervised learning methods, such as the Kernel Naïve Bayes classifier. We use the aforesaid approach to calculate the probability of wrongly identifying the topics in the text corpus. Misinterpreted topic results in delay in response needed to combat the evolving situation, and thus, it culminates in the firm's loss.

LDA is a generative probabilistic model for collections of discrete data (e.g., text corpora). LDA is a three-level hierarchical Bayesian model. It is modeled, such as each item of a collection is a finite mixture over an underlying set of topics. Each topic is, in turn, modeled as an infinite mixture over an underlying set of topic probabilities. In the context of text modeling, the topic probabilities provide an explicit representation of a document (Blei *et al.*, 2003).

$$p_{topic} = f\_clustering\ (Similarity(Topic, Keyword))$$

4.1.4.1.2. Kernel Naïve Bayes classifier (Classification)

On the other hand, kernel-based Naïve Bayes (KNB) classifier Bayesian classifiers are statistical classifiers used to predict class membership probabilities (i.e., the probability that a given dataset record belongs to a particular class). The class with the highest probability is the dominant class for the record. The Naïve Bayes classifier with inherently independent attributes has higher accuracy than those with dependent features (Hastie et al., 2009).

$$p = P(C_i = T_1, T_2, \ldots, T_7 \mid X = K_1, K_2, K_3) \text{ where } K_i = \text{Keyword n-grams}$$

4.1.4.2. Cyber-risk Quantification (CRQ)

The proposed model's next stage deals with quantifying the cyber-risk viz-a-viz expected loss calculation. The expected loss indicates the severity of the DDoS attack in terms of monetary loss to the firm. According to Sharma and Mukhopadhyay (2020), a firm loses US$ 2.14 million for the DDoS attack lifecycle (Sharma and Mukhopadhyay, 2020c). We use this information to calculate loss and subsequently expected loss, that is, the product of the probability of attack with the loss incurred due to attack.

4.1.4.3. Cyber-risk Mitigation (CRM)

The final module suggests ways to mitigate risk and expected loss due to misinterpretation of topic clusters in the text corpus. The decision-maker can either reduce, accept, or pass the cyber-risk by using a combination of financial and technological interventions.

Table 4.4 describes the proposed methodology's steps to generate classification accuracy for correctly identifying key topic clusters in a text corpus. The model then calculates the expected loss and suggests mitigation strategies to reduce losses. We use MATLAB 2021a to analyze the data.

Table 4.4: Steps in the TCRAM model

Step 1	Pre-process the text corpus.
Step 2	Generate topic clusters using a topic modeling algorithm (LDA).
Step 3	Calculate accuracy (p) of detecting topic cluster correctly by using the classifier: $p = KNB\ (topic\_features,\ topic\ cluster\ label)$ (Eq. 1)
Step 4	Expected loss, $E(L) = (1-p) * 2.14$ (Eq. 2)
Step 5	Propose mitigation strategies (technology, cyber-insurance) If $(1-p) > 0.18$ AND $E(L) > US\$\ 0.4$ million, then implement Technology + Cyber-insurance (Eq. 3)

4.2. Smart Cities

We undertake two studies in the context of cyber-risk management frameworks for smart cities. The studies differ in the approach of the methods involved, such as time-series forecasting and deep learning models. They also contrast in the use of structured and unstructured data. We propose two frameworks, namely, SCRAM and DL-CRAM. SCRAM uses structured time-dependent data, while DL-CRAM uses unstructured data such as images to quantify and mitigate cyber-risk. Figure 4.2 gives an overview of studies about smart cities.

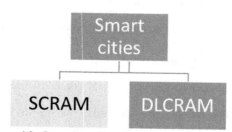

Figure 4.2: Overview of studies related to smart cities

4.2.1. SARIMA-based cyber-risk assessment and mitigation model for a smart city's traffic management systems (SCRAM)

4.2.1.1. Cyber-risk Assessment (CRA)

The ITMS sensors record the average speed of passing vehicles hourly for the nine months described above. We usually observe that the speeds at a particular hour correlate with the same hour's speed on the previous day. We plot ACF values to verify the same for our data, as shown in figure 4.3. We observe autocorrelation at lag 1 and seasonality at lag 24, concurring with earlier studies.

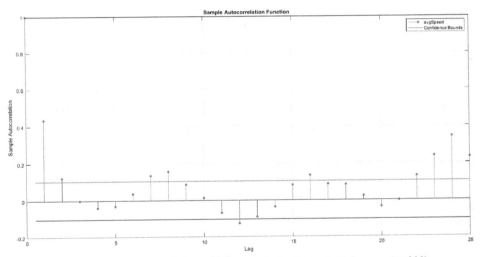

Figure 4.3: ACF plot of the average speed of vehicles in February (n=111)

As shown in table 4.5, we observe that monthly time-series for the nine months mentioned above are stationary and have seasonality at the 24th hour of the day.

Table 4.5: Stationarity and Seasonality test for an average speed of vehicles

Months	Stationarity	Seasonal Lag at 24 hours
Feb	Y	Y
March	Y	Y
April	Y	Y
May	Y	Y
June	Y	Y
August	Y	Y
September	Y	Y
October	Y	Y
November	Y	Y
Feb	Y	Y
March	Y	Y

Therefore, we use a Seasonal Autoregressive Integrated Moving Average (SARIMA) method (Geurts et al. 1977; Gujarati 2009) in order to forecast the average speed as follows:

$$\text{velocity\_of\_vehicle}_t = c + \beta * \text{velocity\_of\_vehicle}_{t-24} + \varepsilon_t \dots\dots\dots(5)$$

where c = constant, velocity_of_vehicle = average speed of vehicles as recorded by ITMS sensors, $\varepsilon_t = t^{th}$ error term

In the next sub-module, we use the anomaly detection method (refer to Equation 6) to compute the proportion of velocities greater than ±2σ vis-a-vis the total number of average velocities in the testing dataset for a particular month.

$$P_{anomaly} = n_{anomaly} / n_{total} \dots\dots\dots\dots\dots\dots\dots\dots\dots\dots\dots\dots\dots\dots\dots\dots\dots(6)$$

where $n_{anomaly} = n_{anomaly} + 1$, if $(\text{velocity}_{actual} - \text{velocity\_of\_vehicle}_t) >= \pm 2\sigma$,

n_{total} = total number of average velocity records for the particular month

Thus, the proportion of anomalous average speeds is indicative of the probability of cyberattack-induced distortion in the ITMS sensors. After that, we also observe that beta distribution best approximates the probability of cyberattack-induced ITMS distortions (I B Hossack et al. 1999).

4.2.1.2. Cyber-risk Quantification (CRQ)

Next, we calculate the expected loss due to hacker-induced tampering of ITMS speed sensors for each month using US$ 2.14 million loss per hour of the attack (Mukhopadhyay et al. 2019). The expected loss for each data record is computed, and gamma distribution (Dutta and Perry 2011) is fitted to the same.

4.2.1.3. Cyber-risk Mitigation (CRM)

We plot the expected loss and risk values on a heat matrix to tag scenarios according to levels of criticality. The decision-maker chooses the boundary values dividing the quadrants and strategies decided per the decision-maker's security attitude. Thus, the heat matrix is divided into four quadrants with varying combinations of risk-severity values. We suggest ways by which smart city administrators can accept, reduce, or pass the cyber-risk by using robust technology and financial interventions (Böhme 2005; Kesan et al. 2013; Majuca et al. 2006; Rejda 2007).

4.2.2. Cyber-risk Assessment and Mitigation framework for smart cities: A deep learning approach (DL-CRAM)

4.2.2.1. Cyber Risk Assessment (CRA)

This study used a convolution neural network (CNN) for the digit recognition submodule (refer to figure 4.4). First, we train the network using the three convolution layers with max-pooling and the ReLU function to adjust for nonlinearity. Then, the probability of correctly identifying a digit is estimated using pixel values of the digit's image as inputs in the CNN model.

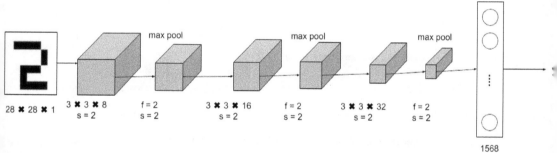

Figure 4.4: Convolutional Neural network for digit recognition

The loss or error of CNN decreases with each epoch. The stopping criterion is the final iteration. When we change certain parameters, it results in poorer performance. Thus, the version presented in this study was the best one out of all the runs (Kunreuther 1997b; LeCun et al. 1989). Table 4.6 details the methodological flow of this study.

Table 4.6: Steps in the DL-CRAM Model

Step 1	**Cyber-risk Assessment (CRA):** *Input*: Two-digit Speed limit sign *Output*: y(Digit 0 to 9) — *Generates a confusion matrix*
Step 2	Calculate 'p' and 'q'. Risk_misclassifying_two_digit_numbers (r)
Step 3	**Cyber-risk Quantification (CRQ)** $E(L) = r * |speed_{predicted} - speed_{actual}|$
Step 4	**Cyber-risk Mitigation (CRM)** *If* r = *Hi* AND $E(L)$ = *Hi, then Self-protection* *Else if* r = *Lo* AND $E(L)$ = *Lo then Cyber-insurance* *Else Self-insurance*

4.2.2.2. Cyber Risk Quantification (CRQ)

In this module, we calculate the opportunity cost, in terms of US$, that a driver/passenger using the autonomous vehicle would lose per year. We used the difference between actual and predicted speed limits as a proxy for loss due to misreading.

4.2.2.3. Cyber Risk Mitigation (CRM)

We plot the expected loss and risk values on a heat matrix to tag scenarios according to levels of criticality. The decision-maker chooses the boundary values dividing the quadrants and strategies decided per the decision-maker's security attitude. Thus, the heat matrix is divided into four quadrants with varying combinations of risk-severity values.

4.3. Crowdfunding platforms

We have used open-source data visualization tools and curve-fitting methods to ascertain the distribution of different variables and their relationships with other numerical variables. Kickstarter encourages campaign organizers to use a large number of images and videos to increase the attractiveness of the campaign. It limits the use of these campaign-specific long descriptions to be used for analysis. Thus, the "blurb" text (short description) along with the title of the campaign serves as an apt data source to analyze what the campaign is promising (Burtch et al. 2013). We also use hierarchical and K-means clustering to find the optimal goal amount. A naive Bayes classifier is used to build a model that will predict the success of campaigns from attributes related to each campaign.

5. Data

This section details the datasets used across the different studies to quantify cyber-risk in digital ecosystems. We use a mix of both structured (such as attack and vulnerability data) and unstructured data (such as text and images).

5.1. Massively Multiplayer Online Gaming (MMOG) platforms

We have proposed four studies pertaining to online gaming platforms. Figure 5.1 details the aforesaid, where we use structured data such as attack and vulnerability data for post-attack analysis. On the other hand, we use unstructured data such as web articles to conduct pre-attack analysis.

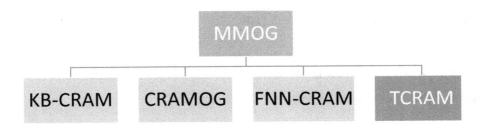

Figure 5.1: Overview of studies related to MMOG platforms

5.1.1. Kernel naïve Bayes classifier-based cyber-risk assessment and mitigation framework for online gaming platforms (KB-CRAM)

We used a dataset of DDoS attacks recorded by a globally reputed content delivery network (CDN) for this study. The dataset contains 10,329 records of DDoS attacks on MMOG firms from 2012 to 2018. Each record of an attack has a start timestamp, end timestamp, bps, packets per second (pps), and attack types (NTP Flood, SSDP Flood, UC, UD, and UDP Flood). We divided the dataset into training (n = 6,197) and testing (n = 4,132) datasets, with a ratio of 60:40. Table 5.1 presents the dataset's summary statistics.

Table 5.1: Summary statistics (2012 Q2 to 2018 Q2)

Attack type	Class	N	Attack trait	Mean	Std. Dev.	Source
UDP Fragment, DNS Flood (UD)	A	3,155	bps (Gbps)	2.7	3.2	
			duration (hours)	19.0	13.8	
NTP Flood	B	2,671	bps	1.1	1.8	
			duration	20.2	14.1	
UDP Fragment, CharGEN Attack (UC)	C	2,030	bps	0.9	1.2	Reputed CDN
			duration	19.9	14.1	
SSDP Flood	D	1,465	bps	0.8	1.3	
			duration	20.8	15.1	
UDP Flood	E	1,008	bps	1.8	4.1	
			duration	19.1	14.3	

Table 5.2 shows that pps and bps are highly correlated, which is why we chose bps to be the sole feature denoting attack intensity.

Table 5.2: Correlation matrix (N=10,329)

Variables	(bps)	(pps)	(duration)
bps	1.000		
pps	0.707***	1.000	
duration	-0.007	0.000	1.000

*** $p<0.01$, ** $p<0.05$, * $p<0.1$

5.1.2. A logit-based Cyber-risk Assessment and Mitigation model for Massively Multiplayer Online Gaming (CRAMOG) platforms

We use data of traits of DDoS attacks on MMOG platforms (i.e., attack intensity and duration) data from a Content Delivery Network (CDN). While we also MMOG platform-specific vulnerabilities from the National Institute of Standards and Technology's (NIST) National Vulnerability Database (NVD) dataset for the specific quarters. As shown in Table 5.3, the CDN dataset contains 10,329 records aggregated into 25 quarters (from 2012 Q2 to 2018 Q2). The dataset comprises five DDoS attacks: NTP Flood, SSDP Flood, UC, UD, and UDP Flood.

Table 5.3: Summary statistics (2012 Q2 to 2018 Q2)

	Variables	N	N_{final}	Attack trait	Mean	Std. Dev.	Source
Attack type	UDP Fragment, DNS Flood (UD)	3,155	23	bps (Gbps)	2.7	3.2	Reputed CDN
				duration (hours)	19.0	13.8	
	NTP Flood	2,671	19	bps	1.1	1.8	
				duration	20.2	14.1	
	UDP Fragment, CharGEN Attack (UC)	2,030	20	bps	0.9	1.2	
				duration	19.9	14.1	
	SSDP Flood	1,465	16	bps	0.8	1.3	
				duration	20.8	15.1	
	UDP Flood	1,008	17	bps	1.8	4.1	
				duration	19.1	14.3	
MMOG platform traits	Vulnerability Score	23,712	25	—	6.2	2.0	NVD feeds
	t* (quarters)	25	25	—	—	—	
	t²* (quarters)	25	25	—	—	—	

| | Vulnerability Count | 23,712 | 25 | — | — | — |

*Training set = 2012 Q2 to 2017 Q1 (20 quarters), Testing = 2017 Q2 to 2018 Q2 (5 quarters), N_{final} = number of quarterly records

Table 5.4 details the correlation matrix of the predictors and target variables in the model.

Table 5.4: Correlation matrix (N = 95)

	p	bps	duration	t	t^2	vulnSc	vC/t	vC/t^2
p	1							
bps	-0.07	1						
duration	-0.03	0.01	1					
t	-0.56***	-0.20**	0.21**	1				
t^2	-0.41***	-0.24**	0.15	0.98***	1			
vulnSc	0.12	0.29***	0.10	-0.60***	-0.69***	1		
vC/t	0.63***	-0.01	-0.18*	-0.51***	-0.38***	0.08	1	
vC/t^2	0.51***	-0.02	-0.17*	-0.37***	-0.26**	0.08	0.95***	1

*** $p<0.01$, ** $p<0.05$, * $p<0.1$

5.1.3. Cyber-risk management framework for online gaming firms: An Artificial Neural Network approach (FNN-CRAM)

This study has used a dataset of DDoS attacks in the MMOG industry captured by a reputed CDN through its cybersecurity service. The dataset contains 10,329 records with six attack attributes each. The attributes, namely bits per second (*bps*), packets per second (*pps*), start timestamp, end timestamp, type of attack, indicate the intensity and duration of the attack and the internet protocol to launch it. The attributes – *bps* and *pps* are highly correlated. Thus, we only use *bps* to gauge the intensity of the attacks. We derive the *duration* of the attack using the start and end timestamp of attacks. Next, we convert attack intensity, the *bps* attribute, into

Gbps (Gigabits per second) and *duration* in hours to adjust for scale variations. The dataset comprises five different DDoS attacks: UC, UD, NTP Flood, SSDP Flood, and UDP Flood. The attack data range from 2012 to 2018. Table 5.5 details the number of records of each kind of DDoS attack.

We aggregate attack records into quarters and years. Thus, for each quarter from 2012 to 2018, we have a total number of attacks and breakdown into five DDoS attacks. We derive the mean attack intensity (in Gbps) and the mean duration of each kind of DDoS attack for each quarter over the same time. Some DDoS attack types do not occur in the initial years, and we have missing values for those attacks, respectively. The pre-processed data informs about the count and kind of DDoS attacks in each quarter and the month of the year. It reduces the volatility in daily data and makes the trend easily discernible (Geurts et al. 1977). CERT and MITRE announce that the vulnerability data only after two quarters (i.e., 180 days) have elapsed since the initial discovery. Thus, the probability of DDoS attacks depends upon this timeline. Therefore, we use the quarterly and monthly aggregates for all the variables to match attack data with vulnerability data (Cavusoglu et al. 2008; Ransbotham et al. 2012).

Table 5.5: Summary statistics for the attack dataset (from 2012 Q2 (t_1) to 2018 Q2 (t_{25}))

Attack type	Count		N_{final}	$D_{training}$	$D_{testing}$		Min	Max	Mean	Std. Dev.
UDP Fragment, DNS Flood (UD)	3,155	Q	23	2013 Q4 to 2017 Q3	2017 Q4 to 2018 Q2	bps	1.5#	28^	3^	3
		M	54	2013 M10 to 2017	2018 M1 to 2018 M2	dur@	0.2	69	19	14
NTP Flood (NF)	2,671	Q	19	2014 Q1 to 2017 Q3†	2017 Q4 to 2018 Q2	bps	112#	19^	1^	2

102

					2018 M1 to 2018 M4	dur@	0.3	69	20	14
		M	45	2014 to 2017						
UDP Fragment, CharGEN Attack	2,030	Q	20	2013 Q3 to 2017 Q2	2017 Q3 to 2018 Q2	bps	0.5#	19^	1^	
		M	54	2013 M9 to 2017	2018 M1 to 2018 M4	dur@	0.1	69	20	14
SSDP Flood	1,465	Q	16	2014 Q3 to 2017 Q3	2017 Q4 to 2018 Q2	bps	363#	22^	1^	1
		M	43	2014 M8 to 2017	2018 M1 to 2018 M4	dur@	0.4	69	21	15
UDP Flood	1,008	Q	17	2012 Q2 to 2017 Q3*	2017 Q3 to 2018 Q2	bps	0#	28^	2^	4
		M	55	2012 to 2017	2018 M1 to 2018 M4	dur@	0.2	68	19	14
N_{total}	10,329									
vulnScore	23,712	25	—	—	—		0	10	6	2
t	25	25	—	—	—		—	—	—	—
t^2	25	25	—	—	—		—	—	—	—
vC	23712	25	—	—	—		—	—	—	—

Training set = 2012 Q2 (t_1) to 2017 Q1 (t_{20}), Testing dataset = 2017 Q2 (t_{21}) to 2018 Q2 (t_{25})

in kbps, ^ in Gbps, *except for 2013 Q4 and 2014 Q1, †except for 2014 Q3, @ duration in hours, Q = Quarterly, M = Monthly

We gather vulnerability time-series data from the National Vulnerability Database (NVD) XML feeds provided by the National Institute of Standards and Technology (NIST). The vulnerability dataset has a publish date, update date, Common Vulnerability Scoring System (CVSS) Score, and vulnerability type. We chose all vulnerabilities of the DoS type for the period matching the DDoS attack timeline (i.e., 2012 Q2 to 2018 Q2). As mentioned earlier, the data is aggregated quarterly and monthly for the years. We choose the number of vulnerabilities and the average vulnerability scores for the same period as additional variables of attack probability. An unpatched vulnerability can also result in multiple DDoS attacks if vendors do not mend before hackers know about them.

5.1.4. Text mining-based cyber-risk assessment for DDoS attacks and mitigation using cyber-insurance (TCRAM)

We use a sample of a text corpus of web articles returned when using "DDoS" as the search term. On average, these documents are 25 lines long. We describe the documents in token types (such as letters, digits, and others.) and named-entity tags (such as a person, location, organization, non-entity, and others). Predominately, tokens are letters and do not belong to any discernible entity. Figure 5.2 summarizes the different token types.

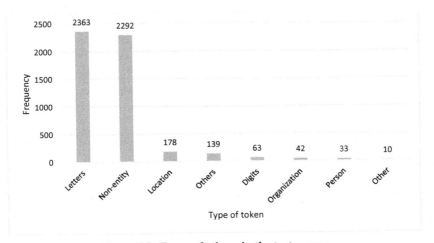

Figure 5.2: Types of tokens in the text corpus

5.1.4.1. Cyber-risk Assessment (CRA)

As shown in figure 5.3, the data suggest that firms across service industries (e.g., BFSI, Entertainment, Cloud Service) are prone to DDoS attacks. It leads to alienation of customers and loss of business reputation. In order to counter it, they spend a substantial amount of their IT budget on perimeter security solutions to reduce the probability of DDoS attacks (D'Arcy et al., 2020; Dhillon and Backhouse, 2000).

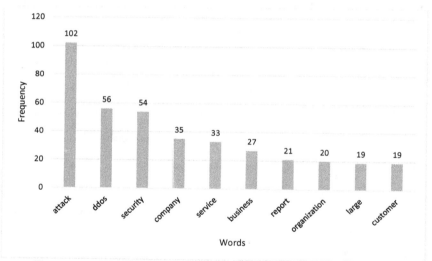

Figure 5.3: Frequency chart for most frequent words in the text corpus

Figure 5.4(a) depicts the word cloud for negative sentiment words in our text corpus. We observe that the firms across three industries (e.g., BFSI, Entertainment, Cloud Service) tend to spend a substantial amount of their IT budget on perimeter security solutions to reduce the probability of DDoS attacks (D'Arcy et al., 2020; Dhillon and Backhouse, 2000). It also highlights the probable attack mechanism, such as obsolete unsecured protocols like UDP,

ICMP, and TCP., exploited by hackers (Sharma and Mukhopadhyay, 2020b; Tanenbaum and Wetherall, 2010). In the event of a DDoS attack, the top management plays an integral part in allaying the fears of the firm's customers and employees.

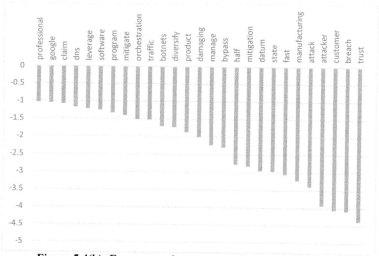

Figure 5.4(a): Word cloud on negative sentiment words

Figure 5.4(b): Frequency chart on negative sentiment words

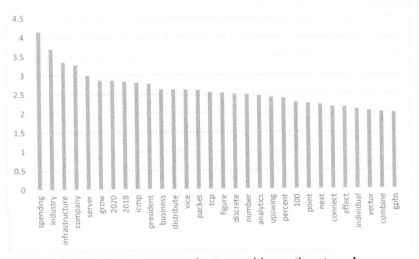

Figure 5.5(a): Word cloud on positive sentiment words

Figure 5.5(b): Frequency chart on positive sentiment words

Figure 5.5(a) illustrates the word cloud for positive sentiment words in our text corpus. We observe that that firms should prioritize cyber-risk mitigation strategies based on attack size. It helps win back customer loyalty (Campbell *et al.*, 2003; Das *et al.*, 2012; Tripathi and Mukhopadhyay, 2020). This aids in preventing customer alienation (Angst *et al.*, 2017). It also suggests that considering analytics-based intelligent mitigation strategies (Mukhopadhyay *et al.*, 2019) with attack size (Tripathi and Mukhopadhyay, 2020) is crucial to robust cyber-risk mitigation.

5.1.4.2. Cyber-risk Quantification (CRQ)

In order to calculate the expected loss due to misinterpretation of themes from web articles, we use loss statistics mentioned by Sharma and Mukhopadhyaya (2020) that states that firms lose US$ 2.14 million ($\mu=2.14$, $\sigma = 0.94$) for each DDoS attack lifecycle (Sharma and Mukhopadhyay, 2020c).

5.2. Smart Cities

We undertake two studies in the context of cyber-risk management frameworks for smart cities. Figure 5.6 depicts them as follows:

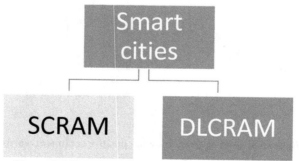

Figure 5.6 Overview of studies related to smart cities

5.2.1. SARIMA-based cyber-risk assessment and mitigation model for a smart city's traffic management systems (SCRAM)

This study uses a dataset from Citypulse, a company that manages smart city projects in Scandinavian countries (Auger et al. 2017; Puiu et al. 2016; Rabhi et al. 2018). The current dataset consists of data collected from a traffic monitoring system in the Danish city of Aarhus. These sensors collect data every 5 minutes about the number of vehicles that passed, average speed, median & average time in the last observation window. As shown in table 5.6, we analyze the 5077 hourly average speed of vehicles across nine months (i.e., February to November, excluding July).

Table 5.6: Descriptive statistics of hourly average speed of vehicles (N_{total} = 5077)

Months	Days	Hours	speed$_{min}$	speed$_{max}$	speed$_{mean}$	speed$_{stdDev}$
February	16	373	28	100	60.94	8.95
March	30	712	29	96	61.04	8.35
April	30	719	15	97	61.23	7.74
May	31	737	29	99	61.12	8.53
June	9	198	29	86	61.84	8.21
August	31	734	32	95	59.97	7.69
September	30	716	25	105	59.63	9.35
October	25	592	21	132	59.01	9.87
November	13	296	26	87	58.42	9.34
Total	215	5077				

Table 5.7 shows we have divided the dataset in the ratio of 70:30 for training and testing, respectively.

Table 5.7: Description of training and testing for SARIMA model

Months	$N_{training}$	$N_{testing}$	N_{total}
Feb	262	111	373
March	499	213	712
April	504	215	719
May	516	221	737
June	139	59	198
August	514	220	734
September	502	214	716
October	415	177	592
November	208	88	296
Total	3559	1518	5077

5.2.2. Cyber-risk Assessment and Mitigation framework for smart cities: A deep learning approach (DL-CRAM)

Table 5.8 shows the composition of the modified dataset generated from MNIST digit recognition dataset (LeCun et al. 1989). Our dataset has 10,000 images made from 28 x 28 pixels of ten digits, 0, 1, up to 9. We randomly chose 60% of these complete images as our training set. Next, we make fundamental transformations to the remaining 40% of the images and distort them by adding noise or removing random pixels from them.

Table 5.8: Dataset composition

Digit	Training	Testing	Digit	Training	Testing
ZERO	600	400	FIVE	600	400
ONE	600	400	SIX	600	400
TWO	600	400	SEVEN	600	400
THREE	600	400	EIGHT	600	400
FOUR	600	400	NINE	600	400

Training (N= 6000), Testing (N=4000)

5.3. Crowdfunding platforms

We have used projects' data on the Kickstarter platform from January 2016 to April 2019. It has a mix of 317,929 fundraisers, out of which we study only 265 successful campaigns and 187 failed campaigns. The campaigns fall within 15 categories (e.g., art, comics, and technology) and 144 sub-categories (e.g., science fiction, television). We analyze the numerical variables that inform us about the pledged amount, goal amount, number of funders, creation date, and state change date. We also collect the campaign's creator data by running a python script to scrape the data. We collect data about the number of campaigns backed and created by the creator, number of friends, and followers of the creator if they have a Twitter profile. In the preprocessing stage, we calculate the duration of the campaign rather than working on the instances in time. Subsequently, we also try to analyze textual data from the title of the projects. We divide the dataset in the ratio of 70:30 for subsequent training and testing by the Kernel naïve Bayes classifier. Table 5.9 summarises the statistical quantities about campaign attributes.

Table 5.9: Descriptive Statistics of the reduced dataset (n=447)

Variables		Count	Min	Max	Mean	Std. Dev.
goalAmount		447	10	293000	16001	33050
pledgedAmount		447	1	777032	16609	63345
duration		447	3	91	33	13
projectTitleLength		447	3	82	36	16
backers_count		447	1	6891	166	505
backerRatio		447	1	5319	104	335
numBacked		447	0	257	9	23
numCreated		447	0	52	2	5
follower_count	without Twitter	250				
	with Twitter	197	0	163394	2201	13651
friend_count	without Twitter	250				
	with Twitter	197	0	19483	353	1754
state	success	265				
	failed	182				

Table 5.10 shows the correlation matrix between the dependent and independent variables.

Table 5.10: Correlation Matrix for variables (n=447)

		(1)	(2)	(3)	(4)	(5)	(6)	(7)	(8)	(9)	(10)	(11)
GA	(1)	1										
PA	(2)	0.40***	1									
DUR	(3)	0.07	0.025	1								
PTR	(4)	0.03	0.15***	-0.03	1							
BCN	(5)	0.18***	0.72***	-0.06	0.08*	1						
BCR	(6)	0.44***	0.35***	-0.03	0.08*	-0.01	1					
NMB	(7)	-0.08*	0.02	-0.12***	0.04	0.14***	-0.04	1				
NMC	(8)	-0.06	0.01	-0.20***	0.07	0.11**	-0.01	0.50***	1			
FLC	(9)	-0.02	-0.01	-0.03	0.06	-0.01	-0.01	0.27***	0.31***	1		
FRC	(10)	-0.03	-0.01	-0.06	0.02	-0.01	-0.01	0.01	0.03	0.16***	1	
STATE	(11)	-0.14***	0.19***	-0.13***	0.15***	0.23***	0.14***	0.24***	0.16***	0.08*	0.08*	1

*** $p<0.01$, ** $p<0.05$, * $p<0.1$

GA = goalAmount, PA = pledgedAmount, DUR = duration, PTR = projectTitleLength, BCN = backers_count, BCR = backerRatio, NMB = numBacked, NMC = num_created, FLC = follower_count, FRC = friend_count

Figure 5.7 illustrates the dendrogram for the original dataset, which was split into 6 clusters. After visualizing the same, we removed three clusters with five outliers data points. Thus, our dataset was reduced to 447 data points subsequently split into 3 clusters, as shown in figure 3.

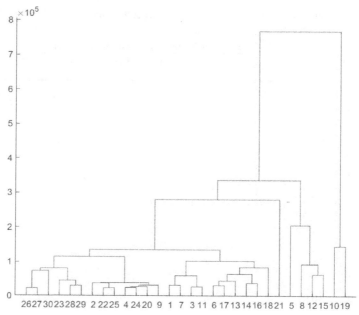

Figure 5.7: Dendrogram for the original dataset (n=452)

As shown in figure 5.8(a), Cluster 1 is the most populated, and thus, the centroid of the same can be used to summarise the optimal goal amount and duration of the campaign in days. Campaigns have an optimal goal amount of US$ 127500 and run for approximately 32 days to become successful.

As shown in figure 5.8(b), the pledged amount follows an exponential distribution with a mean pledged amount of US$ 16,609. The plot for the distribution follows an exponential decay pattern which suggests that most of the campaigns gather smaller pledge amounts. There is a significantly less number of campaigns with higher pledge amounts. Extremely high pledge amounts for campaigns are rare.

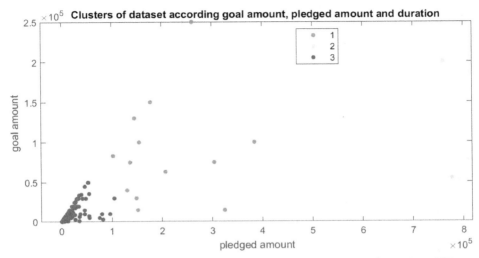

Figure 5.8(a): Clustering after removing outliers from the original dataset (n = 447)

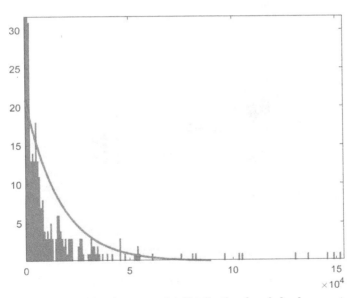

Figure 5.8(b): Fitted exponential distribution for pledged amount

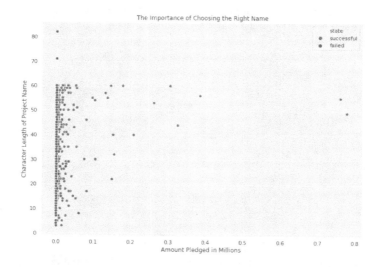

Figure 5.9(a): Campaign title length Vs. Amount pledged by backers

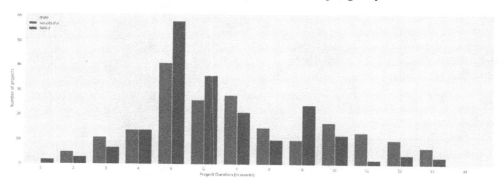

Figure 5.9(b): Number of projects V/s Project Duration (in weeks)

Figure 5.9(a) illustrates that most campaigns have 5 to 6 weeks of duration. The failed to successful projects ratio is almost 1 for projects shorter than 12 weeks. As mentioned in answer to research question 2, campaigns with longer duration attract more funds, but that does not guarantee success. On the other hand, campaigns with smaller duration are moderate to highly successful. We also observed, as opposed to common wisdom, which states that the title of any entity marketed towards consumers (here funders) plays an essential role in deciding its viability in the market, the length of the campaign title does not correlate with the funds pledged to a campaign, as shown in figure 5.9(b).

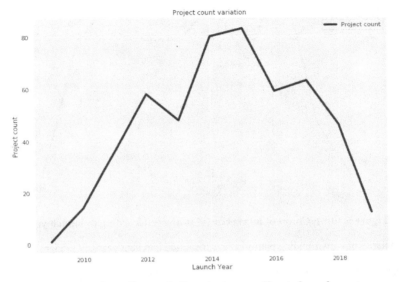

Figure 5.10(a): Count of all projects according to launch year

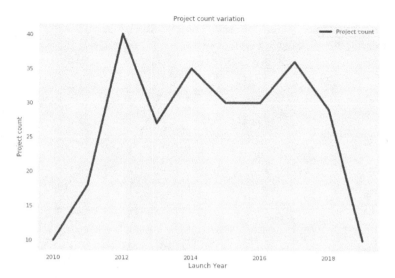

Figure 5.10(b): Count of all successful projects according to launch year

The popularity of crowdfunding platforms has increased in recent years, as evident from figure 5.10(a), where the total number of projects hosted on such platforms has increased since 2012. On the other hand, the total number of successful campaigns on crowdfunding platforms has increased initially but plateaued since 2012-13, as shown in figure 5.10(b).

Creator-specific traits

A founder has a greater chance of attracting funders if they have created and backed many projects on *Kickstarter*. Founders who backed many campaigns had many followers on Twitter, thus, illustrating the interaction between internal and external network effects.

Campaign-specific traits

Campaign-specific traits entail campaign details such as its title, duration, goal amount, pledged amount, and the number of backers. These traits inform us about the intensity and velocity of funds being accrued for a particular campaign.

6. Results

This section details the results of the studies arranged under different modules of cyber-risk management — assessment, quantification, and mitigation across ecosystems such as MMOG platforms, smart cities, and crowdfunding platforms.

6.1. Massively Multiplayer Online Gaming (MMOG) platforms

We have proposed four studies pertaining to online gaming platforms. Figure 6.1 depicts them as follows:

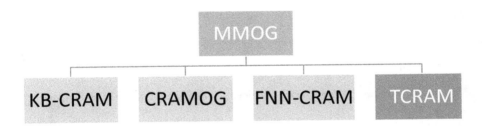

Figure 6.1: Overview of studies related to MMOG platforms

6.1.1. Kernel naïve Bayes classifier-based cyber-risk assessment and mitigation framework for online gaming platforms (KB-CRAM)

The following sections discuss the results for computing the probability (p) of detecting a DDoS attack using the model, the expected loss ($E[L]$) if the model fails to detect the attack vector, and subsequent risk mitigation strategies.

6.1.1.1. Cyber-risk Assessment (CRA)

Our KNB classifier produced a classification accuracy of 80% on the original testing dataset (see Table 6.1).

Table 6.1: Probability of Correct Classification for Testing Dataset (n=4,132)

	Predicted class					
	A	B	C	D	E	p_{attack}
Actual A	1,084	9	167	0	2	0.86
Actual B	8	1,032	0	2	5	0.99
Actual C	140	4	675	0	0	0.82
Actual D	76	165	0	332	5	0.57
Actual E	72	151	11	9	183	0.43

p_{attack} = probability of detecting DDoS attacks

As shown in Figure 6.2(a), the first round of splitting breaks the class E DDoS attacks into three sub-classes and delivers an accuracy of 80.04%. We identified the E1, D, and C classes for splitting through the bottom-up approach. To improve the class-wise model accuracy, we visualize class C using the dendrogram diagram in the last iteration, as shown in Figure 6.2(b).

We observed that classes A and B did not exhibit an additional increment in overall model accuracy (Han et al., 2017). Table 6.2 shows the confusion matrix after the last iteration of the clustering and classification. Diagonal elements (shaded) represent instances in which the model classified attacks correctly (3,553 out of 4,132 records). The model classified 96% of class B attacks and 100% of class E3 attacks correctly. For classes E12 and C2, the model had the lowest overall accuracy rates, 6%, and 25%, respectively. Thus, the CRA module assigns value to the cyber-risk due to DDoS attacks in the form of the attack class's misclassification rate (i.e., $1-p_{attack}$). Figure 6.2 depicts the dendrogram diagram for classes E and C, respectively.

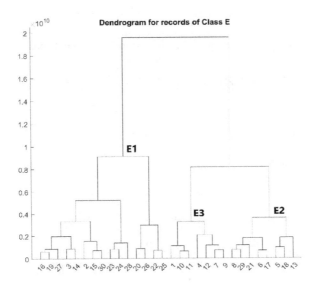

Figure 6.2(a) : Dendrogram for splitting Class E

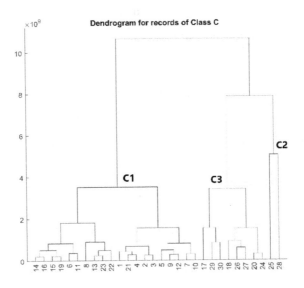

Figure 6.2(b) : Dendrogram for splitting Class C

Table 6.2 details the confusion matrix after last iteration of the cyber-risk assessment algorithm.

Table 6.2: Probability of Correct Classification for Testing Dataset (n=4,132)

Predicted Class

	A	B	C1	C2	C3	D1	D2	D3	E11	E12	E13	E14	E2	E3	p_{attack}
A	1,055	0	187	0	0	0	0	0	0	0	0	0	0	13	0.84
B	6	1,041	0	0	0	2	17	5	0	1	0	0	10	2	0.96
C1	37	2	608	0	5	0	0	0	0	0	0	0	0	0	0.93
C2	3	0	0	1	0	0	0	0	0	0	0	0	0	0	0.25
C3	48	0	0	0	94	0	0	0	0	0	0	0	0	0	0.66
D1	18	16	0	0	0	462	2	0	1	0	1	0	0	0	0.92
D2	5	0	0	0	0	0	52	0	0	0	0	0	3	0	0.87
D3	1	0	0	0	0	0	0	4	0	0	0	0	0	0	0.80
E11	23	0	0	0	1	0	2	0	12	0	0	3	0	0	0.29
E12	10	0	0	0	0	0	4	0	0	1	0	0	1	0	0.06
E13	0	79	1	0	0	2	0	0	0	0	149	2	0	0	0.64
E14	13	10	24	0	0	10	0	0	0	0	0	28	0	0	0.33
E2	7	1	0	0	0	0	1	0	0	0	0	0	28	0	0.76
E3	0	0	0	0	0	0	0	0	0	0	0	0	0	18	1.00

p_{attack} = probability of detecting DDoS attacks

Table 6.3 details the kernel naïve Bayes classifier's different performance metrics in the last iteration of the hybrid CRA module.

Table 6.3: Performance Metric for each DDoS attack class*

Type	Precision	Recall	F1-Score	Type	Precision	Recall	F1-Score
A	0.86	0.84	0.85	D3	0.44	0.80	0.57
B	0.91	0.96	0.93	E11	0.92	0.29	0.44
C1	0.74	0.93	0.83	E12	0.50	0.06	0.11
C2	1.00	0.25	0.40	E13	0.99	0.64	0.78
C3	0.94	0.66	0.78	E14	0.85	0.33	0.47
D1	0.97	0.92	0.95	E2	0.67	0.76	0.71
D2	0.67	0.87	0.75	E3	0.55	1.00	0.71

*After the last iteration

6.1.1.2. Cyber-risk Quantification (CRQ)

In Table 6.4, column 2 demonstrates the risk (i.e., probability of not detecting an attack [1-p]) of each DDoS attack type, while column 3 illustrates their severity (i.e., the expected losses for each attack class). The CRQ module underscores that attacks of class C2 incurred significant losses (of up to US $11.4 million) for MMOG firms. These losses result in MMOG firms firing employees or freezing hiring due to strained budgets. Further, this translates into losing creative talent, which may have strengthened game development. Thus, DDoS attacks may increase delays for upgrades in games, usually for small startups (Kanat et al. 2018).

Table 6.4: Risk-Expected Loss Matrix[#]

Type	(1-p)	E(L) (in millions)	Type	(1-p)	E(L) (in millions)
A	0.16	1.5	D3	0.20	1.8
B	0.04	0.3	E11	0.08	6.9
C1	0.07	0.7	E12	0.13	9.8
C2	0.75	11.4	E13	0.20	3.5
C3	0.34	3.2	E14	0.08	5.8
D1	0.08	0.8	E2	0.24	2.5
D2	0.13	1.5	E3	0.00	0.0

[#]After the last iteration

6.1.1.3. Cyber-risk Mitigation (CRM)

As shown in Figure 6.3, the CRM module generated a heat matrix that situated the different DDoS attacks in the risk × severity quadrants. The finer sub-classes are often undetected by popular classification algorithms as they have attack attributes (such as intensity and duration) similar to those of other DDoS types, thereby, increasing the false positive and false negative rates. The finer sub-classes are interpreted as different ranges for attack intensity and attack duration: high, medium, or low values. Thus, the correct identification of DDoS attacks aids in (i) robust monitoring of vulnerabilities being exploited by hackers and (ii) accurate prediction of probability of being breached by a DDoS attack and its impact thereof. Based on the aforesaid, the CTO can decide the appropriate ways to transfer, reduce, or accept the cyber-risk (Rejda 2007; Zhao, Xue, and Whinston 2013; Mukhopadhyay et al. 2019). Based on which, CTO might decide appropriate mix of technological interventions (such as firewalls, anti-virus, etc.) and financial instruments (such as cyber-insurance).

For example, C2 and E12 DDoS attacks are in the high-risk/high-severity quadrant, E11 and E14 DDoS attacks are in the high-risk and low-severity quadrant, while the remaining are in the low-risk and low-severity quadrant. Thus, the CTO of a firm at risk of C2 and E12 DDoS attacks should consider implementing self-protection measures. Technological interventions such as stringent firewalls, intrusion detection systems, or diversion of excess or illegitimate traffic to backup servers or CDNs can reduce firms' vulnerability against DDoS attacks and lower the attacks' severity (Akamai 2015; Das et al. 2019). Additionally, it is possible to transfer the residual risk by subscribing to cyber-insurance policies, further reducing the risk of being targeted by DDoS attacks and the attacks' severity (Kesan et al. 2013, 2005; Majuca et al. 2006; Rejda 2007).

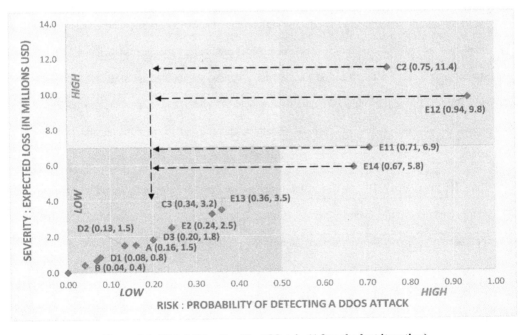

Figure 6.3: Risk Mitigation Heat Matrix (After the last iteration)

6.1.2. A logit-based Cyber-risk Assessment and Mitigation model for Massively Multiplayer Online Gaming (CRAMOG) platforms

This section details the results from the three stages of this study. The first stage takes predictors as input and generates probability values and distribution for each DDoS attack type. The second stage estimates the expected loss and its distribution. The last stage suggests ways to mitigate the cyber-risk in each DDoS attack type.

6.1.2.1. Cyber-risk Assessment (CRA)

GLM based method estimates probability by fitting non-linear patterns from different predictors and squeezing the output within 0 and 1. It measures the proportion of attacks in a quarter of a year (Chen et al. 2011). It is interesting to note that the sign of coefficients in the GLM model informs us about the effect of different predictors in deciding their efficacy and prediction strength. The relationship between model predictors varies across different DDoS attack types. Table 6.5 tabulates the coefficients, p-values, standard errors of the GLM based (i.e., logit and probit) models. We note that models M1 and M2 are significant on the chi-square goodness-of-fit test for each DDoS attack (p-value<0.01) (McCullagh and Nelder 1989).

Table 6.5 shows that NTP attacks are significant for the duration, t, t^2, vC/t, and vC/t^2. These attacks tend to be of low intensity, and short duration yet causes a high impact on MMOG firms ($\beta_{duration}$ = -0.05, p<0.1) (Tanenbaum and Wetherall 2010). Thus, cybersecurity spending reduces the number of vulnerabilities in the short term, but hackers find new ways to attack as its effect fades (Ransbotham et al. 2012). The number of attacks increases in the short term but decreases in the long term. MMO games rely on real-time player involvement, and thus, disrupted time synchronization results in a gamer's reduced performance or even defeat. This type of DDoS attack is quite commonly available in DDoS-for-hire markets to be launched on rival players to take the lead (Herzberg 2016).

Table 6.5: Coefficients of logit and probit models
(Training set = 2012 Q2 to 2017 Q1, i.e., 20 quarters)

		Logit Model (M1)					Probit Model (M2)				
		Coeff.	SE	t	p	Dev.	Coeff.	SE	t	p	Dev.
NTPFLOOD	β_0	-29.00***	5.02	-5.78	0.00	12***	-16.08***	2.76	-5.83	0.00	12***
	bps	-0.01	0.06	-0.14	0.89		-0.01	0.03	-0.28	0.78	
	dur	-0.05*	0.03	-1.72	0.09		-0.03*	0.02	-1.69	0.09	
	t	2.78***	0.60	4.64	0.00		1.52***	0.34	4.45	0.00	
	t^2	-0.07***	0.02	-4.35	0.00		-0.04***	0.01	-4.12	0.00	
	vulnSc	0.22	0.21	1.07	0.29		0.14	0.12	1.18	0.24	
	vC/t	-0.09**	0.04	-2.58	0.01		-0.05**	0.02	-2.47	0.01	
	vC/t^2	2.18***	0.62	3.53	0.00		1.19***	0.34	3.49	0.00	
SSDPFlood	β_0	6.78@	4.58	1.48	0.14	27***	4.38#	2.69	1.63	0.10	27***
	bps	-0.24	0.23	-1.06	0.29		-0.13	0.14	-0.90	0.37	
	dur	-0.06***	0.02	-3.71	0.00		-0.03***	0.01	-3.49	0.00	
	t	-0.56	0.65	-0.86	0.39		-0.42	0.37	-1.15	0.25	
	t^2	0.01	0.02	0.63	0.53		0.01	0.01	0.94	0.35	
	vulnSc	-0.09	0.23	-0.39	0.69		-0.01	0.12	-0.11	0.91	
	vC/t	-0.02	0.05	-0.37	0.71		-0.01	0.03	-0.23	0.82	
	vC/t^2	0.17	0.86	0.20	0.84		0.04	0.52	0.09	0.93	
UC	β_0	-5.08	3.41	-1.49	0.14	36***	-2.58	2.02	-1.28	0.20	36***
	bps	-0.05	0.22	-0.24	0.81		-0.01	0.13	-0.11	0.91	
	dur	0.03#	0.02	1.60	0.11		0.02#	0.01	1.67	0.10	

	Variable	Coeff	SE	z	p	Dev	Coeff	SE	z	p	Dev
	t	1.29**	0.60	2.15	0.03		0.69*	0.35	1.97	0.05	
	t^2	-0.05**	0.02	-2.46	0.01		-0.02**	0.01	-2.29	0.02	
	vulnSc	-0.82***	0.22	-3.78	0.00		-0.46***	0.12	-3.82	0.00	
	vC/t	-0.04#	0.02	-1.64	0.10		-0.02	0.01	-1.50	0.13	
	vC/t^2	0.61*	0.34	1.82	0.07		0.32	0.20	1.63	0.10	
UD	β_0	4.12	7.14	0.58	0.56	34***	1.76	4.09	0.43	0.67	34***
	bps	0.10	0.08	1.23	0.22		0.05	0.05	1.14	0.26	
	dur	0.02	0.03	0.85	0.40		0.01	0.02	0.76	0.45	
	t	-1.14	0.98	-1.16	0.25		-0.57	0.56	-1.02	0.31	
	t^2	0.04#	0.03	1.47	0.14		0.02@	0.02	1.34	0.18	
	vulnSc	0.22	0.21	1.07	0.29		0.11	0.12	0.93	0.35	
	vC/t	-0.04	0.03	-1.19	0.23		-0.03@	0.02	-1.38	0.17	
	vC/t^2	0.28	0.62	0.46	0.65		0.22	0.36	0.62	0.53	
UDPFlood	β_0	-0.85	4.66	-0.18	0.86	12***	-0.68	2.42	-0.28	0.78	12***
	bps	-0.11#	0.07	-1.52	0.13		-0.04@	0.03	-1.42	0.15	
	dur	-0.04	0.03	-1.27	0.20		-0.01	0.01	-1.13	0.26	
	t	-1.14#	0.69	-1.64	0.10		-0.60#	0.36	-1.66	0.10	
	t^2	0.04*	0.02	2.00	0.05		0.02**	0.01	2.03	0.04	
	vulnSc	0.84***	0.28	2.98	0.00		0.44***	0.14	3.21	0.00	
	vC/t	0.01	0.02	0.50	0.62		0.01	0.01	0.42	0.68	
	vC/t^2	0.10	0.32	0.30	0.76		0.07	0.17	0.43	0.67	

Coeff. =Coefficients, Dev.=deviance, dur=duration, vulnSc. =Vulnerability score

*** $p<0.01$, ** $p<0.05$, * $p<0.1$, # $p<0.15$, @ $p<0.2$

SSDP Flood attacks with low duration occur quite frequently ($\beta_{duration}$ = -0.06, p<0.01). This type of DDoS attack targets UPnP devices such as game controllers and game consoles. They can *"zombify"* end-user machines to harm a larger attack surface (e.g., Mirai, Mariposa, and ZBot). Gamers experience delayed response time and may also suffer from financial fraud during DDoS attacks used as a smoke-screen. User Datagram Protocol (UDP) is a stateless protocol; therefore, hackers extensively use it to hide or mislead investigators. UDP Flood DDoS attacks are launched for a shorter duration with or without large attack intensity because this gives hackers a chance to use them as smoke screens. The severity of the vulnerability increases the probability of attack ($\beta_{vulnScore}$ = -0.84, p<0.01).

We test our model (M1) on the last five quarters (i.e., 2017 Q2 to 2018 Q2) and plot an error bar graph at a 95 % significance level (McCullagh and Nelder 1989). UDP Flood attacks have the largest range: [0.31,0.98]. While UC attacks have the smallest range for the last quarter (i.e., 2018 Q2): [0,0.03]. Figure 6.4 depicts the error in predicting the probability of DDoS attacks at a 95 % confidence interval.

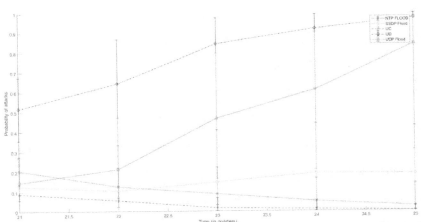

Figure 6.4: Residual analysis of predicted probability (M1) for each DDoS attack (Time: 2017 Q2 to 2018 Q2)

Table 6.6 records the parameter estimates for beta distribution fitted to the probability of DDoS attacks of each type calculated using logit and probit models (Hossack et al. 1983). We observe that UDP Fragment attacks coupled with DNS Flood DDoS attacks are frequent and need special attention while deciding mitigation strategies. DDoS attacks using NTP servers are less probable, with 10 % of the total attacks.

Table 6.6: Beta parameter estimates for risk distribution

Attack type	a	b	Mean	Std. Dev.
NTPFlood	2.07	18.82	0.10	0.00
SSDPFlood	16.68	93.36	0.15	0.00
UC	0.89	24.36	0.04	0.00
UD	3.72	1.03	0.78	0.03
UDPFlood	1.53	1.79	0.46	0.06

a = Shape parameter, b = Scale parameter

6.1.2.2. Cyber-risk Quantification (CRQ)

Table 6.7 indicates that MMOG firms lose around US$ 6.27 million and US$ 0.34 million due to UD and UC attacks, respectively. These expected losses follow a positively skewed gamma distribution with a long tail (Dutta and Perry 2011). The impact of a less frequent attack can accumulate over time and result in massive losses (Peng et al. 2007b). Thus, if MMOG firms do not routinely check for poisoned DNS servers in their ISPs and CDNs., then they can lose money upwards of US$ 6 million. It translates into them foregoing some game developers as their positions are relatively abundant in the development labor market. A DDoS attack may mean delays for new game updates (i.e., avatars, player moves, and landscapes) and, consequently, gamers' dissatisfaction with MMOG firm.

Table 6.7: Gamma parameter estimates for expected loss distribution

Attack type	α	λ	Mean	Std. Dev.
NTPFlood	1.68	0.55	0.93	0.51
SSDPFlood	410.54	0.00	1.20	0.00
UC	0.69	0.49	0.34	0.17
UD	81.44	0.08	6.27	0.48
UDPFlood	6.00	0.57	3.45	1.98

α = Shape parameter, λ = Scale parameter

6.1.2.3. Cyber-risk Mitigation (CRM)

Figure 6.5 depicts the risk-severity heat matrix for each kind of DDoS attack on the MMOG platform. UD attacks are in the high risk-high expected loss quadrant, while others are in the low-low quadrant. MMOG enterprises at risk for UD attacks should consider implementing self-protection. Technological interventions such as scrubbing centers, firewalls, intrusion detection systems, backup servers, vulnerability discovery, or content delivery networks (CDNs) will detect the DDoS attacks, thus, stopping them before incurring losses. Besides, MMOG enterprises can subscribe to cyber-insurance policies to move into the low-low quadrant. Attack records in the High-Low and Low-High quadrants should decide between cyber-insurance or self-insurance depending upon the budgets for absorbing losses and preference over insurance premiums (Akamai 2015; Das et al. 2019; Kesan et al. 2013, 2005; Majuca et al. 2006; Rejda 2007).

Therefore, firms with a DNS service provider at risk of compromise must allot more cybersecurity funds to buy cyber-insurance and self-protection. It also includes educating game developers about industry compliance rules (e.g., GSA) and best practices to prevent vulnerabilities (or bugs) left in game design and development. They also need to educate and inform gamers (or end-users) to update their operating systems and gaming consoles from time to time to prevent backdoor access to their machines through obsolete protocols and code (Chen et al. 2018; Dang-Pham et al. 2017).

On the other hand, low-risk-low-severity attacks use rare and obsolete protocols such as CharGEN and UPnP to compromise an end-user system. These protocols are outdated that can still make firms lose significantly due to delay in identifying the loophole; thus, mentioned. Severity can serve as a proxy of the ethical temperament of particular DDoS attacks. The higher the amount lost, the higher the concern for unethical use of IT resources to cause outages (Brown 2016).

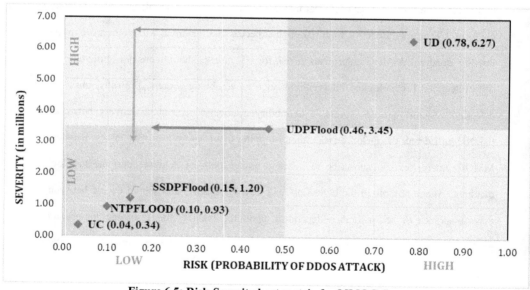

Figure 6.5: Risk-Severity heat matrix for MMOG firm

6.1.3. Cyber-risk management framework for online gaming firms: An Artificial Neural Network approach (FNN-CRAM)

This section details the results from the three stages of this study. The first stage takes variables as input and generates probability values and distribution for each DDoS attack type. The second stage estimates the expected loss and its distribution. The last stage suggests ways to mitigate the cyber-risk in each DDoS attack type.

6.1.3.1. Cyber-risk Assessment (CRA)

As shown in figure 6.6, the training is stopped when validation performance reaches its minimum value in any epoch.

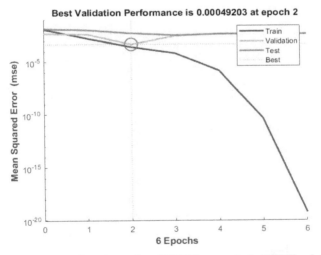

Figure 6.6(a): Performance plot of FNN for quarterly NTPFlood data

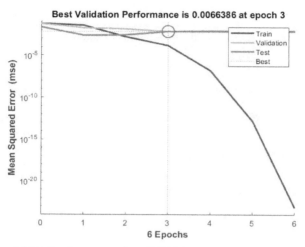

Figure 6.6(b): Performance plot of FNN for quarterly SSDPFlood data

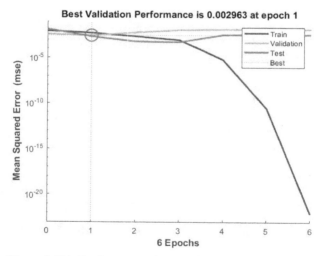

Figure 6.6(c): Performance plot of FNN for quarterly UC data

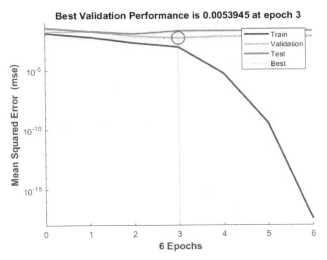

Figure 6.6(d): Performance plot of FNN for quarterly UD data

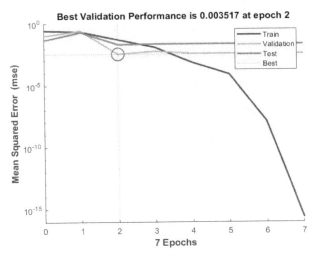

Figure 6.6(e): Performance plot of FNN for quarterly UDPFlood data

Table 6.8 details the mean-squared error performance for each attack across quarterly as well as monthly data. We observe that the mean-squared error for monthly aggregated data is worse off than quarterly aggregation. Moreover, most firms take quarterly budgetary decisions, and thus, the granularity mentioned above matches it (Blau et al. 2019).

Table 6.8: Mean-squared error (MSE) for each attack during training

Attack type	$MSE_{quarterly}$	$MSE_{monthly}$
NTPFlood	0.001	0.005
SSDPFlood	0.003	0.004
UC	0.005	0.007
UD	0.005	0.019
UDPFlood	0.035	0.050

Figure 6.7 compares the actual probabilities of each DDoS attack and computed probabilities from the FNN model after training. Table 6.9 tabulates the performance metric of neural networks for each attack. UD (i.e., combination of UDP Fragment and DNSFlood) attack has the highest test dataset accuracy at 99.76%, as shown in figure 6.7(d). While UC (i.e., the combination of UDP Fragment and CharGEN attack) has the lowest accuracy at 98.76%, as shown in figure 6.7(c). While on monthly data, we have SSDPFlood attacks with the highest test dataset accuracy of 99.78% and the lowest test accuracy of 98.93% for UDPFlood attacks, as shown in figures 9.2 and 9.4, respectively.

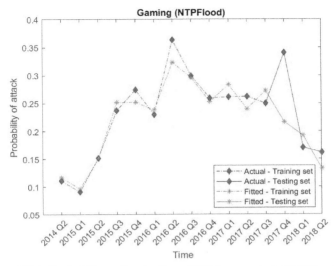

Figure 6.7(a): Probability estimates from FNN for quarterly NTPFlood data

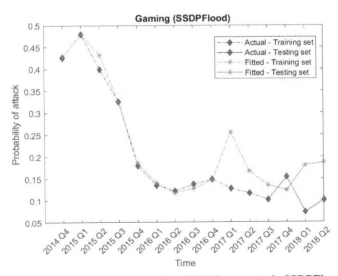

Figure 6.7(b): Probability estimates from FNN for quarterly SSDPFlood data

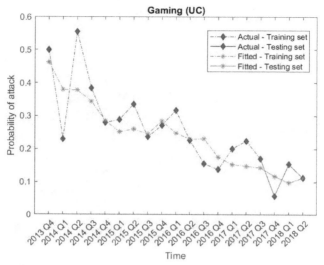

Figure 6.7(c): Probability estimates from FNN for quarterly UC data

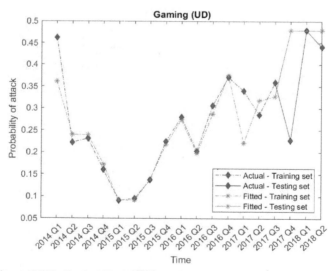

Figure 6.7(d): Probability estimates from FNN for quarterly UD data

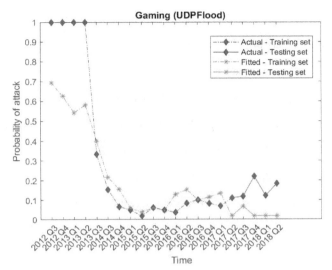

Figure 6.7(e): Probability estimates from FNN for quarterly UDPFlood data

Figure 6.7(e):

Table 6.9 records the computed probability of different DDoS attacks for the testing dataset. UD attacks have the highest probability of occurrence for 2018 Q2, while UC attacks have the lowest probability in 2017 Q4.

Table 6.9: Probability of DDoS attacks for the testing window

Year and quarter	NTP Flood	SSDP Flood	UC	UD	UDP Flood
2017 Q3	—*	—*	0.17	—*	0.12
2017 Q4	0.34	0.15	0.06	0.22	0.22
2018 Q1	0.17	0.07	0.15	0.48	0.12
2018 Q2	0.16	0.10	0.11	0.44	0.18
Test Accuracy (%)	99.74	99.24	98.76	99.76	99.66

* included in the training dataset

We validate and test our FNN model on the last 20% of the records for each attack. Thus, we use the last three quarters of NTPFlood, SSDPFlood, and UD attacks for those mentioned above. Similarly, the last four quarters for UC and UDPFlood attacks serve the same purpose. In all five DDoS attacks, the FNN model correctly estimates the trend in the actual data. Table 6.10 tabulates the parameter estimates of Weibull distribution for risk values along with mean and standard deviations. UD attacks have the highest average risk value at 0.28, while UDPFlood attacks have the lowest average risk values at 0.2 (refer to Table 6.10). The distribution of risk values is positively skewed for SSDPFLood, UC, and UDPFLood attacks, as depicted in Figures 6.8(b), 6.8(c), and 6.8(e). UD and NTPFlood attacks are essentially unskewed, as shown in Figures 6.8(a) and 6.8(d).

Table 6.10: Weibull parameter estimates for risk distribution

Attack type	a	b	Mean	Std. Dev.
NTPFlood	0.24	3.99	0.22	0.004
SSDPFlood	0.26	2.05	0.23	0.014
UC	0.27	2.63	0.24	0.010
UD	0.31	2.51	0.28	0.014
UDPFlood	0.19	0.92	0.20	0.047

a = Shape parameter, b = Scale parameter

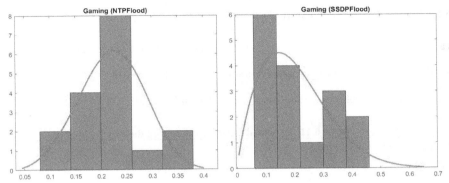

Figure 6.8(a): Weibull distribution for NTP

Figure 6.8(b): Weibull distribution for SSDP

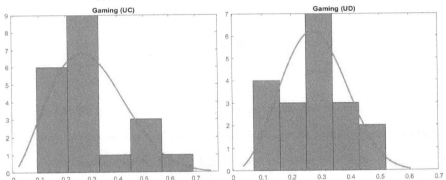

Figure 6.8(c): Weibull distribution for UC

Figure 6.8(d): Weibull distribution for UD

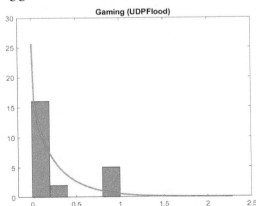

Figure 6.8(e): Weibull distribution for UDP Flood

6.1.3.2. Cyber-risk Quantification (CRQ)

Table 6.11 informs about the expected loss in the testing dataset for five types of DDoS attacks. SSDP attacks have the lowest expected loss at US$ 0.44 million in 2018 Q2, while UD attacks culminate into the highest expected losses at US$ 2.8 million in 2017 Q4.

Table 6.11: Expected Loss for the testing dataset

Year and quarter	NTP Flood	SSDP Flood	UC	UD	UDP Flood
2017 Q3	—*	—*	2.00	—*	2.12
2017 Q4	2.17	0.61	1.60	2.80	1.29
2018 Q1	1.26	0.53	1.27	2.74	1.07
2018 Q2	1.18	0.44	0.98	2.00	1.16

* included in the training dataset

After calculating expected loss values, we fit a gamma distribution on expected loss values. UD attacks have the highest average expected loss at US$ 2.23 million (refer to Table 6.12). In comparison, UC has the lowest average expected loss at US$ 1.83 million (refer to Table 6.12). Figure 6.9 depicts distribution curves for expected loss values. Except for UC attacks, all other attacks' expected losses are positively skewed distributions, as shown in Figures 6.9(a), 6.9(b), 6.9(d), and 6.9(e). Positively skewed distribution hints at the long-tail nature of expected losses. Such distributions have a large number of smaller amounts of expected losses and a very small number of larger expected loss amounts. Thus, DDoS attacks with smaller impacts occur relatively frequently, while severe DDoS attacks are a rarity. The impact of a less frequent attack can accumulate over time and result in massive losses (Peng et al. 2007).

Table 6.12: Gamma parameter estimates for expected loss distribution

Attack type	a	b	Mean	Std. Dev.
NTPFlood	2.06	1.02	2.10	2.14
SSDPFlood	4.66	0.47	2.18	1.02
UC	5.61	0.33	1.83	0.60
UD	3.56	0.63	2.23	1.39
UDPFlood	0.72	2.98	2.15	6.39

Figure 6.9 illustrates the gamma distribution plots for expected loss values.

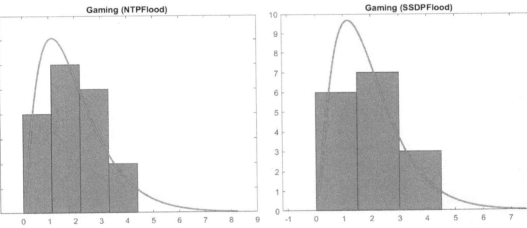

Figure 6.9(a): E(L): Gamma distribution for NTP Flood

Figure 6.9(b): E(L): Gamma distribution for SSDP Flood

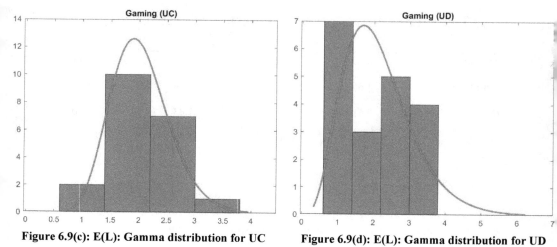

Figure 6.9(c): E(L): Gamma distribution for UC

Figure 6.9(d): E(L): Gamma distribution for UD

6.1.3.3. Cyber-risk Mitigation (CRM)

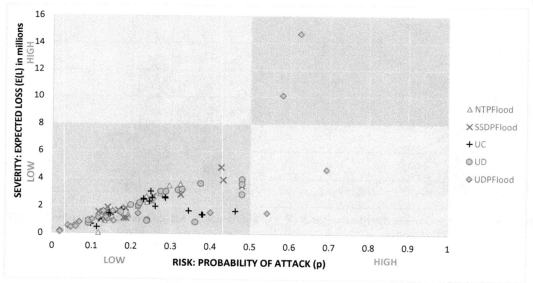

Figure 6.10: Risk-Severity heat matrix

Figure 6.10 depicts the risk-severity heat matrix for each kind of DDoS attack. Each ordered pair on the heat matrix represents the computed probability (p) as computed by the cyber-risk assessment module and expected loss (E(L)), as calculated by the cyber-risk quantification module. Our model will help the CTO accept, reduce, or transfer cyber-risk to a cyber-insurer (Kesan et al. 2013; Kunreuther 1997a; Rejda 2007). UDPFLood attacks are in the high risk-high severity quadrant, with high expected losses, while most other attacks are in the low-low quadrant, with low expected losses. Enterprises at risk for UDPFlood attacks should consider implementing self-protection. Technological interventions such as stringent firewalls or intrusion detection systems or divert excess or illegitimate traffic to backup servers or content delivery networks (CDNs) will decrease the probability of UDPFlood DDoS attacks and thus lower expected losses. Besides, enterprises can subscribe to cyber-insurance policies to move into the low-low quadrant. Attack records in the High-Low and Low-High quadrants should decide between cyber-insurance or self-insurance depending upon the budgets and preference over insurance premiums.

6.1.4. Text mining-based cyber-risk assessment for DDoS attacks and mitigation using cyber-insurance (TCRAM)

6.1.4.1. Cyber-risk Assessment (CRA)

6.1.4.1.1. Traits from web articles

Following the methodology from the previous section, we run the LDA algorithm on the pre-processed text corpus. We use the mix of bigram and trigram models to extract features appropriate from extracting topics from the same. We plotted the validation perplexity score for the different number of topics. We chose the number that gave the lowest perplexity score, i.e., four for the bigram model and three for the trigram model. Figure 6.11 depicts the elbow curve for choosing the optimal number of topics in each case.

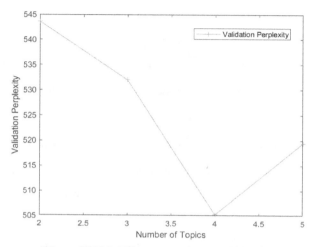

Figure 6.11(a): Elbow curve for bigram model

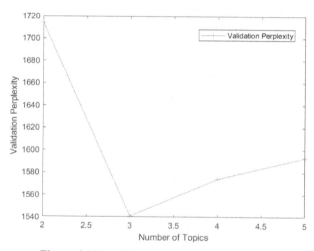

Figure 6.11(b): Elbow curve for trigram model

We group the topic clusters described above under three major themes, namely—cyber-risk assessment (CRA), cyber-risk quantification (CRQ), and cyber-risk mitigation (CRM). Table

6.13 details the top 5 keywords for each topic along with the related cyber-risk management module.

Table 6.13: Top 5 keywords in topic clusters

	Keyword 1	Keyword 2	Keyword 3	Keyword 4	Keyword 5	
Topic 1*	'security solution'	'three industry'	'security service'	'cloud service'	'growth forecast'	CRA
Topic 2*	'network security'	'attack size'	'company infrastructure'	'lost revenue'	'size firm'	CRQ
Topic 3*	'security spending'	'security incident'	'corero network'	'technology category'	'large business'	CRA
Topic 4*	'security professional'	'few month'	'combine icmp'	'research report'	'effect ddos'	CRA
Topic 5#	'customer trust confidence'	'program vice president'	'icmp attacker become'	'udp multiple tcp'	'firm claim attack'	CRA
Topic 6#	'intelligence response orchestration'	'attack firm observe'	'number mitigation neustar'	'loss customer trust'	'attack size firm'	CRM
Topic 7#	'manage security service'	'ddos attack cost'	'spending growth forecast'	'become motivated bypass'	'big attack firm'	CRQ

* = bigram based, # = Trigram based

Cyber-risk Assessment

Figures 6.12(a), 6.13(a), and 6.14(a) show the word clouds for topics 1, 3, and 5. We observe that they belong to the CRA module. Figures 6.12(a) and 6.12(b) inform us that firms across three industries (e.g. BFSI, Entertainment, Cloud Service) tend to spend a substantial amount of their IT budget on perimeter security solutions to reduce the probability of DDoS attacks (D'Arcy et al., 2020; Dhillon and Backhouse, 2000). As shown in figures 6.12(b) and 6.13(b), security solutions ($p_{topic} = 0.025$) and spending ($p_{topic}=0.030$) are essential points for a firm to consider to defend against potential DDoS attacks proactively (McKeay, 2017). Figure 6.14(a) describes the probable attack routes, such as obsolete unsecured protocols like UDP, ICMP, and TCP, exploited by hackers (Sharma and Mukhopadhyay, 2020b; Tanenbaum and Wetherall, 2010). It also suggests that in the event of a DDoS attack, top management plays an integral part in allaying the fears of the firm's customers and employees. Figure 6.14(b) shows that customer confidence and trust ($p_{topic} = 0.03$) is the crucial decision point when assessing risk due to DDoS attacks. At the same time, identification of probable attack mechanisms through protocols such as TCP, UDP, and ICMP ($p_{topic}=0.005$) is essential. Also, the top management commitment ($p_{topic}=0.025$) to minimize DDoS attacks aids in their robust cyber-risk management (D'Arcy et al., 2020).

Topic 1

security analytics
activity report first quarter security purchase
cloud service next five
three industry 100 gpbs
forecast period
security solution
neustar see
point uptick security service
past year
fast spending growth forecast
spending growth large country
bypass defense
size company

Figure 6.12(a): Topic 1

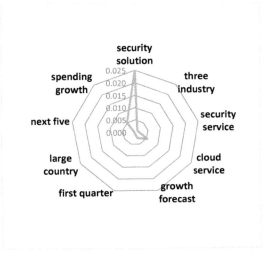

Figure 6.12(b): Topic probability of keywords

Topic 3

intelligence response
integration service three hour attack leverage
respondent two ponemon ibm
technology category
spend billion corero network packet per
security spending
orchestration software
security incident
second large large business per second
enforcement point average cost
automate security
spending guide

Figure 6.13(a): Topic 3

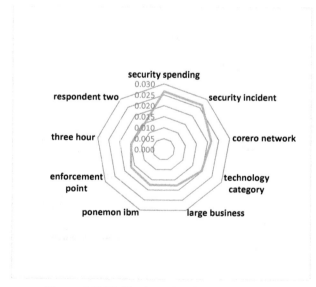

Figure 6.13(b): Topic probability of keywords

customer insight analysis
multiple tcp icmp
security spending guide
firm claim attack something result large
uptick number mitigation
icmp attacker become
ddos attack business   per second traffic
customer trust confidence
bypass defense begin program vice president
second half report udp multiple tcp   see customer deploy
increase average size
motivated bypass defense
hit ddos attack fast spending growth
cost organization 50000

Figure 6.14(a): Topic 5

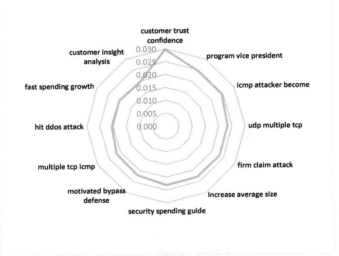

Figure 6.14(b): Topic probability of keywords

Cyber-risk Quantification

Figures 6.15(a) and 6.16(a) represent word clouds for cyber for topics 2 and 7. Figure 6.15(a) highlights that the severity of a DDoS attack is decided by firm size and attack (Sharma and Mukhopadhyay, 2020a; Yue *et al.*, 2019). In comparison, figure 6.16(a) depicts that firms invest in MSSPs to reduce the instances as well as the severity of DDoS attacks (Gupta and Zhdanov, 2012; Kahane *et al.*, 1988). Figure 6.16(a) also highlights that quantification of attack cost is an important metric to gauge the extent of the damage for the firm following a DDoS attack (Gordon *et al.*, 2003; Mukhopadhyay *et al.*, 2013). As shown in figure 6.15(b), network security (p_{topic} = 0.06) and attack size (p_{topic}=0.05) are two important factors to quantify cyber-risk. At the same time, figure 6.16(b) shows that firms subscribe to MSSPs (p_{topic}=0.04) to lower their attack cost (p_{topic}=0.035).

Topic 2

spending industry
cybersecurity product product service
diversify second organization 50000
attack firm company infrastructure manage security
lost revenue
network security
attack vector attack size traffic something
cost organization size firm security 2018
endpoint security udp multiple
disaster recovery
large average

Figure 6.15(a): Topic 2

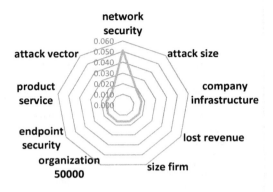

Figure 6.15(b): Topic probability of keywords

connect company infrastructure
security analytics intelligence
traffic something result
discrete manufacturing federal
professional loss customer big attack firm attack size company
clearly upswing big
ddos attack cost
see mitigated high
manage security service
packet per second spending growth forecast
newly distribute workforce   point uptick number
become motivated bypass
tcp icmp attacker
diversify second half
semiannual security spending
analytics intelligence response

Figure 6.16(a): Topic 7

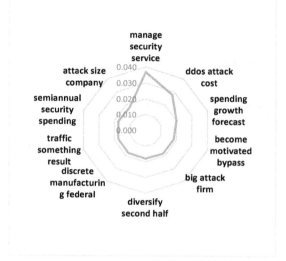

Figure 6.16(b): Topic probability of keywords

Cyber-risk Mitigation

Figure 6.17(a) depicts the word cloud for Topic 6. It deals with cyber-risk mitigation and focuses on intelligent responses to DDoS attacks. As shown in figure 6.17(a), we observe that firms should prioritize cyber-risk mitigation strategies based on attack size. It helps win back customer loyalty (Campbell *et al.*, 2003; Das *et al.*, 2012; Tripathi and Mukhopadhyay, 2020). This aids in preventing customer alienation (Angst *et al.*, 2017). Figure 6.17(b) shows that analytics-based intelligent mitigation strategies (p_{topic} = 0.022) (Mukhopadhyay *et al.*, 2019) with attack size (p_{topic} = 0.021) (Tripathi and Mukhopadhyay, 2020) consideration are crucial to robust cyber-risk mitigation.

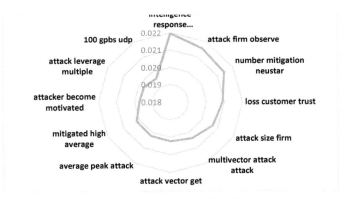

Figure 6.17(a): Topic 6

Figure 6.17(b): Topic probability of keywords

6.1.4.1.2. *Probability of misinterpreting themes in web articles*

Next, we train a Kernel Naïve Bayes classifier on the training dataset with different topic probabilities as the feature vector. We divide the dataset in both bigram and trigram in the ratio of 60:40. Figure 6.18 depicts the ROC curve for trigram model.

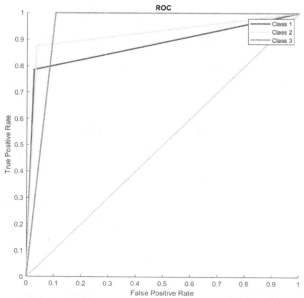

Figure 6.18: ROC curve for trigram model

Table 6.14 details the confusion matrix with topic-wise classification accuracy and overall accuracy (i.e., 89 percent for the bigram model and 90 percent for the trigram model) for those mentioned earlier. Diagonal elements (shaded) represent instances in which the model correctly classified attacks (i.e., 70 out of 78 in the bigram model 47 out of 52 in the trigram model). Topic 4 is the best classified at 96 percent accuracy, while topic 2 is the worst classified at 67 percent accuracy.

Table 6.14: Confusion Matrix for Testing Dataset

Topic Label	T1	T2	T3	T4	Total (N = 78)	Probability of detecting topic (p)
T1	15	1	0	0	16	0.93
T2	1	10	2	2	15	0.67
T3	0	1	20	0	21	0.95
T4	0	1	0	25	26	0.96
	T5	T6	T7		Total (N = 52)	
T5	12	0	1		13	0.92
T6	1	16	2		19	0.84
T7	1	0	19		20	0.95

T_i = i^{th} topic cluster, where i = 1,2,...,7

6.1.4.2. Cyber-risk Quantification (CRQ)

We posit that topic misinterpretation delays risk quantification. Thus, it prolongs the DDoS attack and resulting in losses for the firms. Misinterpretation of topic 2 incurs the most considerable amount of expected loss at US$ 0.69 million. We note that expected loss values follow a long-tail distribution (Dutta and Perry, 2011). In this study, we observe that expected losses due to misinterpretation follow a gamma distribution (a = 1.99, b = 0.12, μ = 0.24, σ = 0.17) (Mukhopadhyay *et al.*, 2019). Figure 6.19 depicts the gamma distribution curve for expected losses.

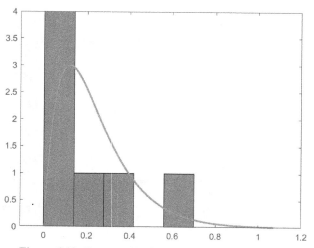

Figure 6.19: Gamma distribution for the expected loss

6.1.4.3. Cyber-risk Mitigation (CRM)

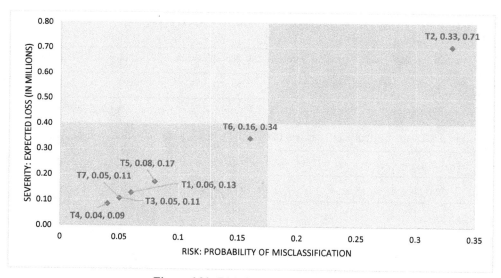

Figure 6.20: Risk-Severity heat matrix

Figure 6.20 depicts a heat matrix that situates the different attack classes regarding Risk × Severity. Topic 2 is in the high risk- high expected loss quadrant, while other topics are in a low risk - low expected loss quadrant. Firms at risk of misinterpreting or delaying information processing should implement the following mitigation strategies. The Chief Technology Officer (CTO) should implement a highly accurate threat intelligence system with more comprehensive data sources and better text mining algorithms. Human tagging of topic clusters can also improve the accuracy of the classifier. It aids in better understanding the cyber-attack landscape's evolving situation. Thus, increasing the probability of detecting correct themes attacks and lowering expected losses due to delayed or wrong response orchestration. If a firm fails to identify topics in the low-low quadrant, they can directly subscribe to cyber-insurance due to the low-risk premium. Otherwise, firms can use a combination of technological intervention and cyber-insurance policies to move into the low-low quadrant (Das *et al.*, 2019; Herath and Herath, 2011; Kesan *et al.*, 2013; Mukhopadhyay *et al.*, 2019; Rejda, 2007).

6.2. Smart Cities

We undertake two studies in the context of cyber-risk management frameworks for smart cities. Figure 6.21 depicts the aforesaid.

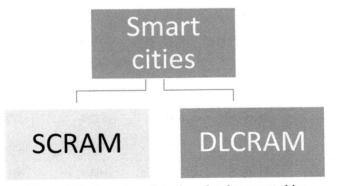

Figure 6.21: Overview of studies related to smart cities

6.2.1. SARIMA-based cyber-risk assessment and mitigation model for a smart city's traffic management systems (SCRAM)

6.2.1.1. Cyber-risk Assessment (CRA)

Table 6.15 shows the SARIMA model results for each month and the number of anomalous data points detected by the methodology, where columns 2 to 5 are based on equation 5, while column 6 on equation 6. The probability of an attack is calculated as the proportions of anomalous data points in the total data points for that month, based on column 6. Columns 4 and 5 indicate the AIC and BIC values used to ascertain the goodness of fit of the SARIMA model for each months' data.

Table 6.15: SARIMA model parameters

Month	Constant (c)	β	AIC	BIC	$n_{anomaly}$
(1)	(2)	(3)	(4)	(5)	(6)
February	34.14	0.44	780.9	780.9	9
March	38.20	0.38	1448.0	1448.0	8
April	39.04	0.36	1476.5	1476.5	15
May	41.11	0.32	1545.6	1545.6	13
June	35.65	0.41	393.3	393.3	2
August	44.23	0.26	1489.0	1489.0	15
September	29.68	0.51	1512.0	1512.0	14
October	49.54	0.17	1285.6	1285.6	12
November	31.61	0.47	668.6	668.6	12

As shown in figure 6.22(h), in the month of October the current average speed ($velocity_t$) of vehicles is the least dependent ($\beta_{October} = 0.17$) on the previous day's average speed from the same hour (i.e., $velocity_{t-24}$). While, as shown in figure 6.22(j), in the month of November, the current average speed (velocity$_t$) of vehicles is the least dependent ($\beta_{November}$ = 0.47) on the previous day's average speed from the same hour (i.e., velocity$_{t-24}$). At the same time, we observe that monthly time-series have positive drift, highest (c$_{October}$ = 49.54) in October and lowest in September (c$_{September}$ = 29.68). The AIC and BIC values across the nine months highlight that higher value results in a larger number of anomalies due to poor fit across time-series data.

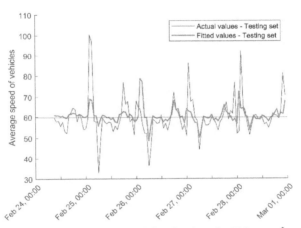

Figure 6.22(a): Actual and fitted values for February[*]

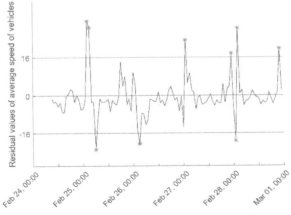

Figure 6.22(b): Anomalous average speeds for February

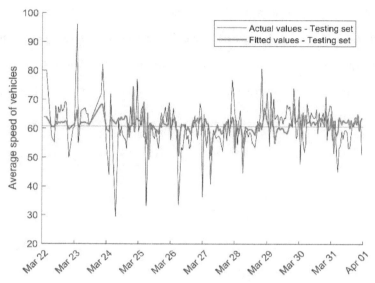

Figure 6.22(c): Actual and fitted values for March*

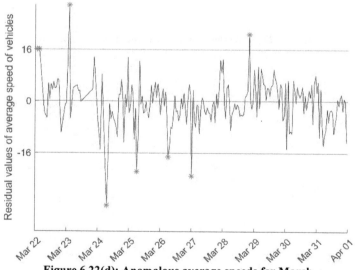

Figure 6.22(d): Anomalous average speeds for March

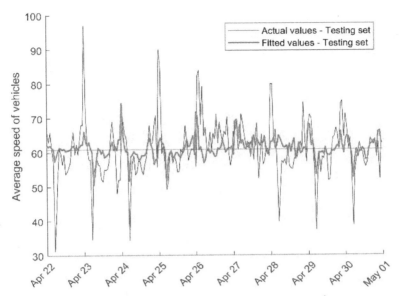

Figure 6.22(e): Actual and fitted values for April

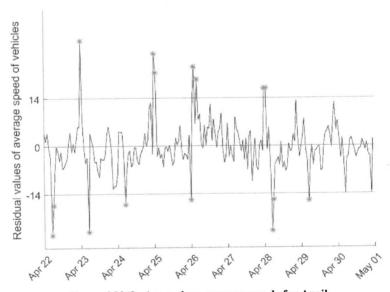

Figure 6.22(f): Anomalous average speeds for April

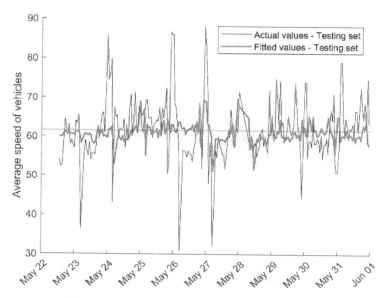

Figure 6.22(g): Actual and fitted values for May*

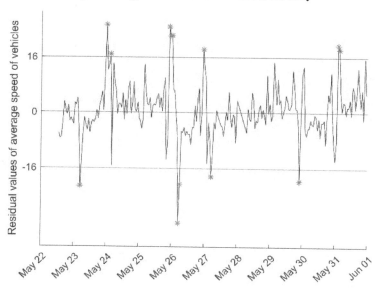

Figure 6.22(h): Anomalous average speeds for May

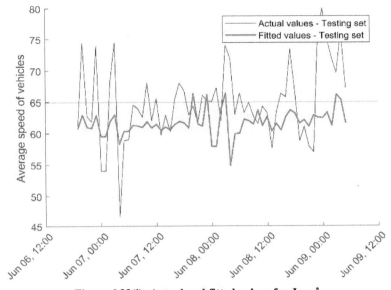

Figure 6.22(i): Actual and fitted values for June*

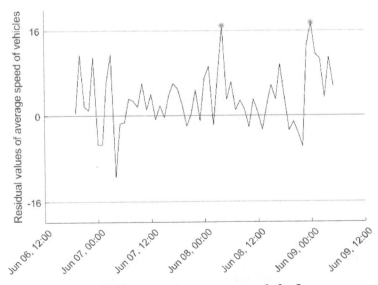

Figure 6.22(j): Anomalous average speeds for June

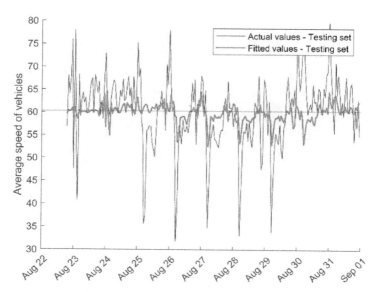

Figure 6.22(k): Actual and fitted values for August

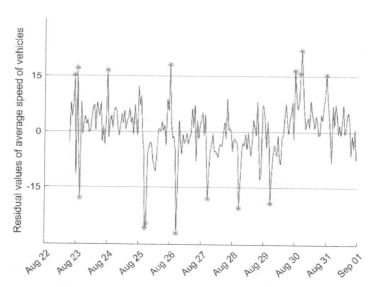

Figure 6.22(l): Anomalous average speeds for August

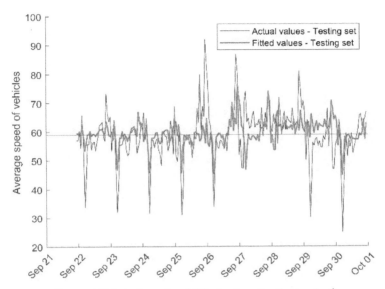

Figure 6.22(m): Actual and fitted values for September*

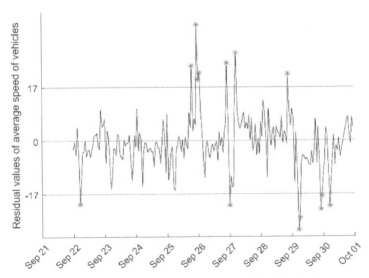

Figure 6.22(n): Anomalous average speeds for September

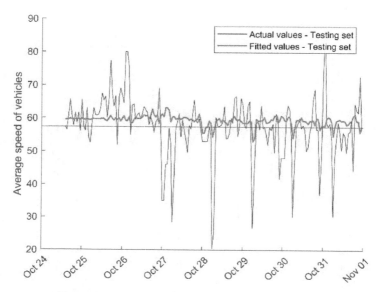

Figure 6.23(o): Actual and fitted values for October

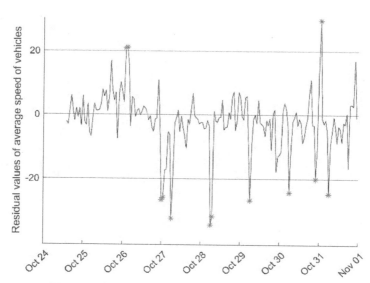

Figure 6.24 p): Anomalous average speeds for October

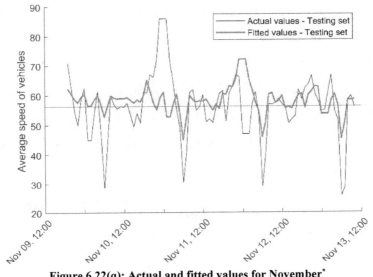

Figure 6.22(q): Actual and fitted values for November*

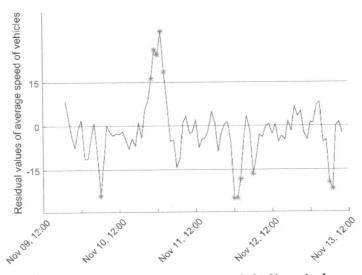

Figure 6.22(r): Anomalous average speeds for November*

As shown in table 6.16 and figure 6.22(r), the month of November has the highest proportion of anomalies and thus, results in a higher probability of cyberattacks. While the summer months, such as April, May, and June, have a lower proportion of anomalies. At the same time, the transition months have a moderate proportion of anomalies. The observed results concur with a difficult commute by vehicles during winter months due to snow and earlier sunsets, which affect road conditions and visibility. We also posit that these months are lucrative for hackers due to increased difficulty in identifying true anomalies from weather-associated anomalous vehicle behavior.

Table 6.16: Probability of mispredicting the average speed from the testing dataset

Month	Overspeed	Underspeed	N	$n_{anomaly}$	$p = n_{anomaly}/N$
February	6	3	111	9	0.08
March	4	4	213	8	0.04
April	7	8	215	15	0.07
May	8	5	221	13	0.06
June	2	0	59	2	0.03
August	8	7	220	15	0.07
September	7	7	214	14	0.07
October	3	9	177	12	0.07
November	5	7	88	12	0.14

Next, we try to ascertain the best distribution to generalize the probabilities values computed in the last module. As shown in figure 6.23, we observe that probability of cyber attack-related anomalies follow a beta distribution (a = 5.8, b = 77.4, μ = 0.07, σ = 0.03) (I B Hossack et al. 1999). Thus, on average, 7 percent of average speeds recorded every hour by the ITMS sensors are anomalies and point to hacker-induced tampering of sensors.

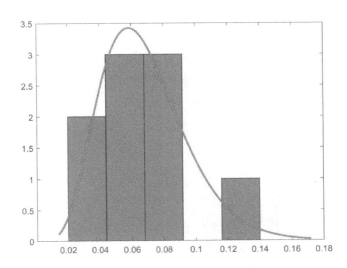

Figure 6.23: Beta distribution curve for the probability of attacks on an ITMS sensor

6.2.1.2. Cyber-risk Quantification (CRQ)

Table 6.17 shows the expected loss for those attack instances (i.e., anomalous data points).

Table 6.17: Expected Loss for each month

Month	p	duration	E(L)
February	0.08	9	1.56
March	0.04	8	0.64
April	0.07	15	2.24
May	0.06	13	1.64
June	0.03	2	0.15
August	0.07	15	2.19
September	0.07	14	1.96
October	0.07	12	1.74

| November | 0.14 | 12 | 3.50 |

As shown in figure 6.24, we observe that the expected loss values follow a gamma distribution (a = 2.1, b = 0.8, μ = 1.7, σ = 1.2) concur with long-tail distribution of losses in extant literature (Dutta and Perry 2011).

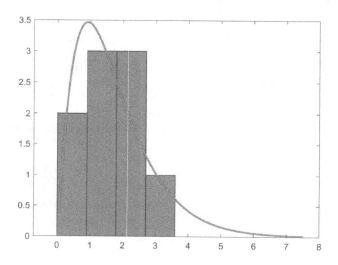

Figure 6.24: Gamma distribution curve for expected loss values due to tampering of ITMS sensor

6.2.1.3. Cyber-risk Mitigation (CRM)

Figure 6.25 shows a heat matrix that plots different months' probability of attack and their expected losses across four quadrants of varying risk severity. November is the riskiest month in terms of cyber-attacks and their effect on congestion on streets. City administrators may follow undermentioned mitigation strategies: (i) Government cybersecurity administration may implement technology (like stringent firewalls, intrusion detection systems or divert excess/illegitimate traffic to backup servers, CDNs) which will help decrease the probability of an cyberattack and thus, lower the expected loss for riskiest months; (ii) Government can now subscribe to cyber-insurance policies and reach the low-low quadrant for riskiest months (Kesan et al. 2013; Majuca et al. 2006; Rejda 2007).

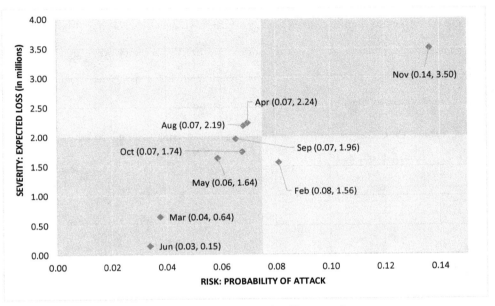

Figure 6.25: Risk Mitigation Heat matrix

6.2.2. Cyber-risk Assessment and Mitigation framework for smart cities: A deep learning approach (DL-CRAM)

6.2.2.1. Cyber Risk Assessment (CRA)

Table 6.18 shows the confusion matrix generated by the CNN model (Accuracy = 97%) for the digit recognition module. Digits 5, 6, and 7 have a 99% detection accuracy, while digit '9' has the lowest accuracy of 92%. Owing to its shape, digit 9 has the highest number of misclassifications and thus confuses it with other digit classes.

Table 6.18: Confusion matrix for the testing dataset using CNN model for digit recognition (n = 4,000)

		Predicted values										$p_{accuracy}$	Rank
		0	1	2	3	4	5	6	7	8	9		
Actual values	0	484	0	2	0	0	0	0	2	1	0	0.99	1
	1	0	488	1	0	1	2	6	4	3	8	0.95	4
	2	3	7	489	0	3	0	0	4	5	2	0.95	4
	3	1	1	1	489	0	1	0	0	3	0	0.98	2
	4	0	3	0	0	493	0	0	0	1	3	0.99	1
	5	0	0	0	3	0	494	1	0	1	0	0.99	1
	6	3	0	0	0	1	1	474	0	0	0	0.99	1
	7	0	1	1	0	1	0	0	489	3	0	0.99	1
	8	4	0	0	5	0	2	4	0	475	0	0.97	3
	9	5	0	6	3	1	0	15	1	8	487	0.92	5
	Overall Accuracy											0.97	

In the subsequent tables, we tabulate the results of estimating the probability and expected loss for the three scenarios using some real-world speed limits.

Only the first digit is incorrectly read (NY scenario)

An autonomous vehicle can misread speed-limit in 447 ways for this type of misidentification. Table 6.19 reports nine of them, the number of overspeeding cases and the mean and standard deviation of the misread speeds. An autonomous vehicle can misread a speed limit of '10' as 20, 40, 50, 60, 70, 80, and 90, all of which are overspeeding cases. The speed limit of 90 has reported eight underspeeding, while the speed limits of 40 and 50 have one each. Also, five original speeds (i.e., 20, 30, 60, 80, and 90) are misread as "00", which results in a slowing of the vehicle, leading to congestion. Similarly, six original speeds (i.e., 10, 20, 30, 40, 50, 70, 90) have been misread as 80, which results in vehicle overspeeding, leading to a collision.

Table 6.19: Speed limit misreading for NY scenario

Speed	00	10	20	30	40	50	60	70	80	90	Mean	Std. Dev.	OS	US
10	—	—	O	—	O	O	O	O	O	O	59	24	7	0
20	U	U	—	—	O	—	—	O	O	O	48	38	4	2
30	U	U	U	—	—	O	—	—	O	O	42	38	3	3
40	—	U	—	—	—	—	—	—	O	O	60	44	2	1
50	—	—	—	U	—	—	O	—	O	—	57	25	2	1
60	U	—	—	—	U	U	—	—	—	—	30	26	0	3
70	—	U	U	—	U	—	—	—	O	—	38	31	1	3
80	U	—	—	U	—	U	U	—	—	—	35	26	0	4
90	U	—	U	U	U	U	U	U	—	—	44	27	0	8
US_m	5	4	3	3	3	3	2	1	1	0				
OS_m	0	0	1	0	2	2	2	2	6	4				
Total	5	4	4	3	5	5	4	3	7	4				

U = Underspeeding, O = Overspeeding, US_m = Misread underspeeding, OS_m = Misread overspeeding

We approximate the frequency of misread speed limits using the normal distribution ($\mu = 4.4$, $\sigma = 1.15$). This implies that speed limits 00, 10, 20, 40, 50, 60, and 90 are the most frequently misclassified, whereas speed limits 30, 70, and 80 are rarely misclassified. Thus, hackers prefer to tamper with speed limits (i.e., 10, 20, 30, 40, 50, 70, and 90), causing the deep-learning algorithm to misread them as 80 (i.e., six overspeeding and one underspeeding case).

Only the second digit is incorrectly read (YN scenario)

An autonomous vehicle can misread speed-limit in 447 ways for this type of misidentification. Table 6.20 reports nine of them. It shows that the original speed limit of '10' can be misread as 12, 17, and 18. We note that the digit '0' in the unit's place can be misread in three ways (i.e., 2, 7, and 8). It leads to overspeeding and colliding with other vehicles. We observe that the misread speeds follow a uniform distribution (a = 0.0116).

Table 6.20: Impact of misreading speeds (YN scenario) (n = 27)

Original Speed	Misread Speed	US	OS	Total	Mean
10	12,17,18	—	3	3	16
20	22,27,28	—	3	3	26
30	32,37,38	—	3	3	36
40	42,47,48	—	3	3	46
50	52,57,58	—	3	3	56
60	62,67,68	—	3	3	66
70	72,77,78	—	3	3	76
80	82,87,88	—	3	3	86
90	92,97,98	—	3	3	96

		Total		0	27

Both digits are incorrectly read (NN scenario)

An autonomous vehicle can misread speed-limit in 2016 ways for this type of misidentification. Table 6.21 reports nine of them. We group speeds into ten triads (i.e., A, B, ..., J), each with three variants corresponding to unit digits 2, 7, and 8.

Table 6.21: Speed limit misreading for NN scenario

Speed	A	B	C	D	E	F	G	H	I	J	Mean	Std. Dev.	US	OS
10	—	—	O	—	O	O	O	O	O	O	59	24	7	0
20	U	U	—	—	O	—	—	O	O	O	48	38	4	2
30	U	U	U	—	—	O	—	—	O	O	42	38	3	3
40	—	U	—	—	—	—	—	—	O	O	60	44	2	1
50	—	—	—	U	—	—	O	—	O	—	57	25	2	1
60	U	—	—	—	U	U	—	—	—	—	30	26	0	3
70	—	U	U	—	U	—	—	—	O	—	38	31	1	3
80	U	—	—	U	—	U	U	—	—	—	35	26	0	4
90	U	—	U	U	U	U	U	U	U	—	44	27	0	8
US_m	5	4	3	3	3	3	2	1	1	0				
OS_m	0	0	1	0	2	2	2	2	6	4				
Total	5	4	4	3	5	5	4	3	7	4				

U = Underspeeding, O = Overspeeding, US_m= Misread underspeeding, OS_m= Misread overspeeding, A = (02, 07, 08), B = (12, 17, 18), C = (22, 27, 28), D = (32, 37, 38), E = (42, 47, 48), F = (52, 57, 58), G = (62, 67, 68), H = (72, 77, 78), I = (82, 87, 88), J = (92, 97, 98)

The five original speeds (i.e., 20, 30, 60, 80, and 90) can be misread as category A, leading to congestion. Similarly, six original speeds (i.e., 10, 20, 30, 40, 50, 70, 90) have been misread as category I, leading to a collision.

We approximate the frequency of misread speed limits using the normal distribution ($\mu = 4.4$, $\sigma = 1.15$). It implies that speed limits A, B, C, E, F, G, and J are the most frequently misclassified, whereas speed limits D, H, and I are rarely misclassified. Thus, hackers prefer to tamper with seven original speed limits (i.e., 10, 20, 30, 40, 50, 70, and 90), causing the deep-learning algorithm to misread them as category I (i.e., six overspeeding and one underspeeding case).

Probability distribution for estimating the likelihood of predicting the speed limit

In continuation, the probability of predicting cases with one digit wrong and both digits wrong follow the Weibull distribution (a = 0.00003, b = 0.94, mean = 0.00004, variance = 0.000000001) (I. B. Hossack et al. 1999).

6.2.2.2. Cyber Risk Quantification (CRQ)

This section discusses expected loss due to autonomous vehicles for the following scenarios.

Only the first digit is incorrectly read (NY scenario)

Figure 6.26(a) shows that the speed limit '90' has the lowest variance in the difference between actual and misread speeds, signifying the lowest expected loss values. The original speed limits of 20 and 30 have relatively high differences and, therefore, higher expected losses in comparison.

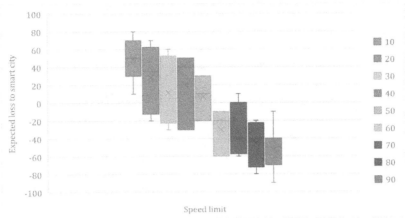

Figure 6.26(a): Expected loss in NY scenario

Both digits are incorrectly read (NN scenario)

Figure 6.26(b) illustrates that the speed limit '90' has the lowest variance in the difference between actual and misread speeds, signifying the lowest expected loss. The original speed limits of 20 and 30 have relatively high differences and, therefore, higher expected losses in comparison.

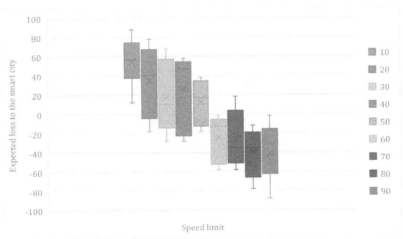

Figure 6.26(b): Expected loss in NN scenario

An autonomous vehicle misreads the two-digit speed limit in 2910 ways. Table 6.22 reports some of these cases. The expected losses are as high as USD 0.5 million in overspeeding compared to USD 0.05 million in underspeeding cases.

Table 6.22: Impact on smart-city due to misreading of speeds

Scenario	Original Speed	Misread Speed	Difference	r	Impact (I)	Outcome
NY	30	80	+50	0.0100	0.500	Collision
NY	70	90	+20	0.0000	0.000	Collision
NY	20	50	+30	0.0000	0.000	Congestion
NY	80	30	-50	0.0010	0.050	Congestion
NY	90	70	-20	0.0100	0.020	Congestion
NY	50	20	-30	0.0000	0.000	Congestion
NN	35	53	+18	0.0001	0.005	Collision
YN	30	38	+8	0.0000	0.000	Collision

Probability distribution for estimating the likelihood of predicting the speed limit

We fit a gamma distribution ($a = 0.6$, $b=0.002$, $\mu= 0.0012$, $\sigma = 0.000002$) to estimate the expected loss for all the scenarios (Becker 1978; Mukhopadhyay et al. 2013). This signifies that small expected losses due to misreading the speed limit signs by autonomous vehicles are quite frequent, while large expected losses for the same vehicles are rare.

6.2.2.3. Cyber Risk Mitigation (CRM)

Figure 6.27 depicts a heat matrix calculated in terms of risk × severity. Speed limit misidentification of type NY is in the high risk-high severity quadrant. Therefore, the smart-city administrator should consider implementing the following risk mitigation strategies. First, add firewalls or intrusion detection systems or block excess/illegitimate traffic to reduce the risk and thus lower the severity of cyber-attacks. Next, transfer the residual risk by self-insuring followed by subscribing to cyber-insurance policies, thus shifting into the low risk-low severity quadrant (Biswas et al. 2017; Han et al. 2017; Scuotto et al. 2016).

Speed limit misreading cases of YN and NN type are situated in the low risk-low severity quadrant. Thus, it can be outsourced to third-party cyber-insurers straight away, as these cases have risk values low enough to be acceptable to cyber-insurance policy providers (Böhme and Schwartz 2006; Han et al. 2017; Majuca et al. 2006; Mukhopadhyay et al. 2019; Rejda 2007).

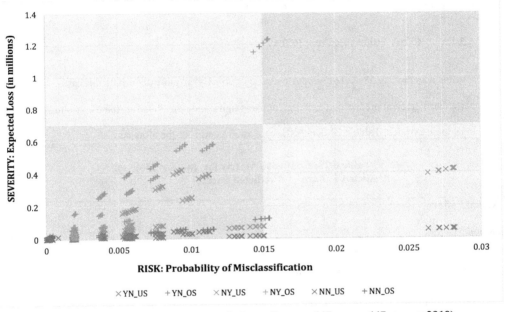

Figure 6.27: Risk-Severity heat matrix (n_{NN} =6, n_{YN} = 447, n_{NY} = 447, n_{total} = 2910)

6.3. Crowdfunding platforms

We observe that the following campaign-specific traits are crucial for the success of crowdfunding campaigns. Campaigns with lower goal amounts are usually more successful than others. Shorter duration campaigns had a higher chance of succeeding as they did not suffer from crowding out effects (Burtch et al. 2013). A higher backer ratio (pledged amount per backer) promotes the success of a campaign due to same-side network effects on the platform. People donate more to seeing other people donate. However, this effect slackens in the case of campaigns with too high a goal amount.

6.3.1. Cyber-risk Assessment (CRA)

Overall accuracy is 58%. The model classifies correctly in more than half the cases. It is particularly good at predicting the failure of campaigns, and thus, those attribute combinations have to be avoided. Table 6.23 details the confusion matrix for the aforesaid.

Table 6.23: Confusion Matrix for ($n_{testing}$=136)

	Predicted Failure	Predicted Success	p	q
Actual Failure	54	2	0.96	0.04
Actual Success	56	24	0.30	0.70

6.3.2. Cyber-risk Quantification (CRQ)

Table 6.24 shows the expected loss calculation for successful and failed campaigns on Kickstarter.

Table 6.24: Risk and Severity values for campaigns ($n_{testing}$ = 136)

(in USD)	Average goal amount	Loss*	Expected Loss
Failure	31,100	1,555	62
Success	3,909	195	137

*Loss of platform fees (i.e., 5% of goal amount)

At the same time, table 6.25 details the risk and impact values for all misclassified campaigns in our test dataset.

Table 6.25: Risk-Impact values for misclassified campaigns

R	I	R	I	R	I	R	I
0.030	2.377	0.003	0.046	0.000	0.003	0.000	0.001
0.001	0.122	0.000	0.000	0.002	0.748	0.004	1.350
0.147	110.325	0.000	0.001	0.008	1.753	0.000	0.005
0.000	0.002	0.000	0.000	0.000	0.000	0.001	0.096
0.001	0.008	0.001	0.041	0.002	0.051	0.000	0.000
0.003	1.630	0.001	0.103	0.006	2.436	0.000	0.025
0.001	0.005	0.000	0.046	0.009	0.916	0.000	0.008
0.000	0.002	0.001	0.187	0.001	0.105	0.002	0.086
0.057	28.566	0.001	0.071	0.000	0.001	0.002	0.057
0.000	0.000	0.001	0.287	0.000	0.001	0.080	19.963
0.000	0.010	0.003	0.768	0.001	0.198	0.000	0.000
0.007	2.719	0.000	0.007	0.000	0.006		
0.001	0.042	0.000	0.000	0.001	0.146		
0.000	0.003	0.000	0.002	0.066	19.826		
0.000	0.045	0.002	0.273	0.001	0.050		

R = 1 - $p_{posterior}$, I = Impact (i.e., Expected Loss)

6.3.3. Cyber-risk Mitigation (CRM)

Figure 6.28 depicts the heat matrix for risk-severity values for misclassified campaigns. To mitigate the cyber-risk due to fraud campaigns, we suggest the following. Firstly, we recommend using consortium blockchain to validate the campaign information before onboarding them on the platform. This procedure will benefit the crowdfunding platforms in two ways. First, they will eliminate campaigns that might result in fraud or failure. Second, it will improve the campaign data quality for future decisions that have to be taken algorithmically. We posit that training data becomes robust after using the blockchain to ensure fraud, tampered, or misinformation-based campaigns are not launched on the platform. This will also enhance the accuracy with which the automated algorithms (such as KNB) identify the success state of any campaign before it launches. Subsequently, the platform can reduce loss of the platform fees due to misclassification of success state of campaigns.

Platforms like Kickstarter and Indiegogo can shift their operations on a consortium-based blockchain network which will help in ensuring that the fund transfers can happen in a trusted environment through encrypted ledger entries. The distributed ledger in blockchain networks makes it easy for people to observe the quantum and velocity of funds being pledged to a particular campaign. Thus, they make an informed choice of pledging to the creditworthy campaigns. This mechanism makes it difficult for the campaign organizers to overstate the success of campaigns and fraud the funders.

Smart contracts on such blockchains will prevent the transfer of funds from backers to founders in cases where the product is never realized after a successful campaign run. The reward-based crowdfunding model can be replicated on a blockchain without even the need for lucrative incentives. The campaign founders can offer ICOs (Initial Coin Offerings), which will convert into an object such as a natural asset, collectible, or any other crypto-asset corresponding to the value of token coins (Chen 2018). The blockchain-based crowdfunding model was first proposed in 2013 and had raised almost $11.4 billion in 2018, from $10 billion during 2017, with a 13 percent growth (Pozzi 2019). Kickstarter alone had helped campaigns collect just $4.4 billion in crowdfunding dollars since its launch in 2009 (Kickstarter 2019). This amount is a fraction of the amount that decentralized platforms have incurred. Blockchain firms such as StartEngine, WeiFund, and CryptStart have been at the forefront of decentralized crowdfunding initiatives. The massive interest in decentralized offerings on the blockchain networks has resulted in swift growth for these firms.

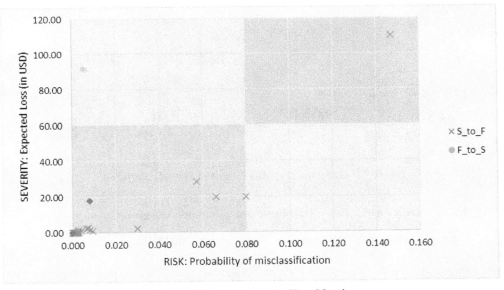

Figure 6.28: Risk-Severity Heat Matrix

7. Discussion

This section discusses the results of the studies in conjunction with extant literature to situate the contributions in the cyber-risk management discourse.

7.1. Massively Multiplayer Online Gaming (MMOG) platforms

We have proposed four studies pertaining to online gaming platforms. Figure 7.1 depicts the aforesaid.

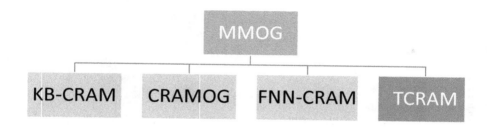

Figure 7.1: Overview of studies related to MMOG platforms

7.1.1. Kernel naïve Bayes classifier-based cyber-risk assessment and mitigation framework for online gaming platforms (KB-CRAM)

This study models the five different kinds of DDoS attacks used mainly by hackers to disrupt network traffic, increase latency, and damage MMOG firm's reputation (McKeay 2017). These DDoS attacks vary in intensity, duration, and overlapping in nature (Peng, Leckie, and Ramamohanarao 2007). Thus, making it difficult to distinguish them and mitigate them. Our KB-CRAM consists of three modules: Cyber-risk Assessment, Quantification, and Mitigation, which aims to identify these DDoS attacks, thereby computing the expected loss for them. Subsequently, it proposes mitigation strategies for the MMOG firm.

The first stage (CRA) of the framework presented in our study addresses cyber-risk assessment, in accordance with previous studies in which risky assets were identified in cyber-enabled firms (Bandyopadhyay and Mookerjee 2019; Biswas and Mukhopadhyay 2018; Das et al. 2019; Gordon et al. 2003; Mukhopadhyay et al. 2019; Sharma and Mukhopadhyay 2020a). We used a kernel naïve Bayes classifier (Han et al. 2017) to predict the probability of each kind of occurrence for different types of DDoS attacks. We used hierarchical clustering with dendrogram visualization followed by k-mean clustering to boost the classifier's accuracy (Hastie, Tibshirani, and Friedman 2009; Han, Kamber, and Pei 2017). We observed that our hybrid CRA module performed well on three performance metrics: precision, recall, and F1-score (Han, Kamber, and Pei 2017).

The second stage (CRQ) of the framework quantified the expected losses (i.e., severity) for each type of DDoS attack for an MMOG platform (Courtney 1977; Das et al. 2019; Mukhopadhyay et al. 2019). In the framework's third stage (CRM), we suggested various strategies to mitigate cyber-risk. CTOs of MMOG firms have the crucial task of choosing mitigation strategies that are not cost prohibitive and that assure appropriate risk hedging during cyberattacks. In this study, we suggest four risk classes under which we mapped different DDoS attack records. CTO should reduce the probability of DDoS attacks featuring in the high-risk and high-severity quadrant by strengthening the firm's cyber-defenses such as firewalls, backup CDNs, and intrusion detection systems (Böhme and Kataria 2006; Chatterjee et al. 2015; Chatterjee 2019; Herath and Herath 2007). Firms experiencing DDoS attacks in high-risk and low-severity quadrant (or low-risk and high-severity) may choose between self-insurance and cyber-insurance depending upon budget availability (Mukhopadhyay et al.

2019). Firms facing DDoS attacks in the low-risk and low-severity quadrant can subscribe to cyber-insurance because their risk premiums are within acceptable limits (Kesan et al. 2013; Majuca et al. 2006; Rejda 2007). This coerces firms to be more mindful of cybersecurity vulnerabilities and its mitigation (Austin and Darby 2003; He and Zhang 2019).

We contribute to the academic discussion by proposing an iterative and hybrid data mining approach with both supervised and unsupervised learning modules. First, we use a supervised learning method, such as KNB, to predict the five types of DDoS attacks. If the overall accuracy is below a certain threshold, we split the most misclassified DDoS attack classes using K-means clustering (Han, Kamber, and Pei 2017). We split these misclassified DDoS attack classes into subclasses by visualizing the data using a dendrogram (Han, Kamber, and Pei 2017). We pass these subclasses to the KNB algorithm again. We repeat this process until the overall accuracy of the KNB classifier was above 90 percent. The KNB classifier outputs the confusion matrix (Han, Kamber, and Pei 2017). Our CRA module computes the final probability of attack subclasses. Subsequently, our CRQ module calculates the expected loss caused by each DDoS attack (Bezsonoff 2017; Mukhopadhyay et al. 2019; Tripathi and Mukhopadhyay 2020). Our CRM module highlights three different scenarios based on varying levels of risk and severity of losses (Rejda 2007; Mukhopadhyay et al. 2013). It suggests whether MMOG firm should opt for self-protection (e.g., technological interventions) and cyber-insurance measures (Zhao, Xue, and Whinston 2013; Kesan, Yurcik, and Majuca 2013).

MMOG firms value latency, scalability, and brand reputation in their business models (Wu and Hsu 2018; Yahyavi and Kemme 2013). Our study contributes to MMOG firms' management strategies in the following ways. First, it provides CTOs with a tool with easy-to-understand steps and actionable cyber-risk management insights to mitigate DDoS attacks in the MMOG industry. The 2×2 cyber-risk mitigation heat matrix provides exact mitigation steps along with probable investment strategies. Thus, managers can measure whether a given firm must invest in technology, cyber-insurance, or both. These mitigation strategies discourage hackers and increase customers' confidence in the firm's offerings.

The current study is limited by its use of anonymized cyberattack data; therefore, firm-level variables were not included in our model. Thus, better datasets with firm-level details can improve the predictability and validity of the model. Using alternate data sources such as forums for hackers and for the online gaming community can help predict imminent DDoS attacks by analyzing hacker behavior. Future research should test this framework in scenarios where attack features are correlated and follow other types of probability distributions.

7.1.2. A logit-based Cyber-risk Assessment and Mitigation model for Massively Multiplayer Online Gaming (CRAMOG) platforms

MMOG industry has been plagued with numerous technical and ethical issues due to its multi-stakeholder business environment. Our CRAMOG model consists of three stages (or modules). The first stage of the framework deals with the cyber-risk assessment, which concurs with prior studies to identify risky assets in a cyber-enabled firm (Bandyopadhyay and Mookerjee 2019; Biswas and Mukhopadhyay 2018; Das et al. 2019; Gordon et al. 2003; Mukhopadhyay et al. 2019; Sharma and Mukhopadhyay 2020). We have used GLM based model to predict the probability of each kind of DDoS attack. Newer vulnerabilities in the software and hardware make it difficult to predict the proportion of attacks. We concur with earlier studies that highlighted cyber-assets with vulnerabilities enable higher incidences of cyber-attacks (Gordon et al. 2003; O'Reilly et al. 2018). Thus, our study's platform-specific traits, such as vulnerability counts and trends, serve as significant predictors and chief risk enabling components. We found that short-duration DDoS attacks targeted on MMOG firms were more likely to occur than long-duration variants (Biswas and Mukhopadhyay 2018; Mukhopadhyay et al. 2019;

Tanenbaum and Wetherall 2010). We also found that a decrease in the number of vulnerabilities due to cybersecurity spending by MMOG firms resulted in lesser incidences of DDoS attacks (Arora et al. 2008; Kannan and Telang 2005). The results also indicate that cybersecurity spending reduces the number of vulnerabilities in the short-term, but hackers find new ways to attack as its effect fades (Arora et al. 2008; Ransbotham et al. 2012; Safi et al., 2021). Attackers use these vulnerabilities to compromise the cyber-assets, and thus, monitoring and removing these bugs helps reduce cyber-attacks (D'Arcy et al. 2020). Subsequently, we establish that the probability of DDoS attack in the MMOG industry follows a beta distribution, as pointed by earlier studies estimating the distribution of failure in computer systems (Mukhopadhyay et al. 2019).

The second stage of the framework quantifies losses for each kind of DDoS attack. Our study uses expected loss as a proxy for the severity of DDoS attacks (Courtney 1977; Mukhopadhyay et al. 2019). We concur with prior studies establishing that expected losses due to DDoS follow gamma distribution in the MMOG industry (Das et al. 2019; Dutta and Perry 2011; Mukhopadhyay et al. 2019).

The third stage of the framework suggests ways to mitigate cyber-risk. CTOs of the MMOG firms have a crucial task in choosing mitigation strategies that do not bleed into profits and assure appropriate risk hedging when under cyber-attacks. In this study, we suggest four risk classes under which we have mapped different DDoS attack records. Attacks under high risk and high severity scenarios have to reduce their cyber-risk by subscribing to self-protection (Böhme and Kataria 2006). Self-protection entails developing firewalls, backup CDNs, and intrusion detection systems (Böhme and Kataria 2006; Herath and Herath 2007). Prior studies have shown that it is easier to discourage hackers by strengthening the firm's cyber-defenses rather than deciphering different ways hackers attack cyber-systems (Chatterjee et al. 2015).

Attacks falling in high risk-low severity or low risk-high severity have a choice between self-insurance and cyber-insurance. They have to choose between the substitutes depending upon the availability of budget, and in comparison, they would have paid as risk premium (Mukhopadhyay et al. 2019). Low risk-low severity attacks can straightaway subscribe to cyber-insurance because risk premiums are within acceptable limits. The extreme risk class (Hi-Hi) has to treat self-protection and cyber-insurance as compliments (Kesan et al. 2013; Majuca et al. 2006; Rejda 2007). The practice of subscribing to Self-insurance or cyber-insurance disciplines the internal working of product development teams. It coerces them to be mindful of cybersecurity flaws and vulnerabilities that might otherwise make it susceptible to attacks (Austin and Darby 2003).

We contribute to the academic discussion by suggesting a novel predictor and framework for cyber-risk management in the MMOG industry. Our study contributes in the following ways. We treat cyber-risk management as a tool to reduce ethical concerns for MMOG firms emanating from hackers. Our study is one of the first studies to quantify and mitigate cyber-risk in MMO games using logit-probit models. The proposed model uses both attack-specific and MMOG platform-specific traits in quantifying cyber-risk. We also introduce novel predictors incorporating a decreasing trend in vulnerabilities due to cybersecurity spending for quantifying cyber-risk. Lastly, we suggest cyber-insurance coupled with self-protection as a viable method to mitigate cyber-risk in the MMOG industry due to DDoS attacks.

MMOG firms value latency, scalability, and brand reputation as drivers of revenue. Our study has the following managerial implications. First, it provides CTOs with a tool with easy-to-understand steps and actionable insights in the form of cyber-risk management to mitigate DDoS attacks in the MMOG industry. The 2×2 cyber-risk mitigation heat-matrix provides exact mitigation steps along with probable investment strategies. Thus, managers could gauge whether the firm needs to invest in technology, cyber-insurance, or both. These mitigation strategies will discourage the hackers from causing financial loss to the firm and increase customers' confidence in the authenticity of MMOG firms' offerings.

The current study is limited by using a proxy for cybersecurity spending. The MMOG firms strategically guard the actual data about the cybersecurity budget, and thus, its availability would improve the model's prediction quality. We have used anonymized cyber attack data; therefore, firm-level variables do not form part of the model. Better datasets with firm-level details will improve the predictability and validity of the model further. Using alternate data sources such as hacker forums and online gaming community discussions can help predict imminent DDoS attacks by incorporating a sliver of hacker behavior.

7.1.3. Cyber-risk management framework for online gaming firms: An Artificial Neural Network approach (FNN-CRAM)

This study focuses on the cyber-risk management of DDoS attacks in the MMOG industry. The MMOG industry has faced 74% of the total attacks in 2018-2019 (McKeay 2017). Gaming firms not only suffer monetary losses due to disrupted gameplay, but cyber-attacks damage their reputation amongst end-users, who have scalability, low latency, and immersive experience as the top demands (Wu and Hsu 2018). The model proposed in the paper consists of three stages (or modules). The first stage of the framework deals with the cyber-risk assessment. We have used Feedforward neural network (Han et al. 2017) to compute the probability of each kind of DDoS attack. Newer vulnerabilities in the software and hardware make it difficult to compute the proportion of attacks. Our model incorporates attack features along with vulnerability counts and severity. On average, it takes 180 days for a vulnerability to be publicly disclosed by an agency such as CERT (Ransbotham et al. 2012). Thus, hackers can exploit the vulnerabilities from the previous quarter and launch zero-day attacks based on the currently exposed vulnerabilities. Therefore, our model incorporates the independent variables from the previous quarter, improving its accuracy. We also include the interaction effect of the dependence of vulnerabilities trends over time. Neural networks can fit non-linear functions over data efficiently, making them indispensable for computing the probability of attacks for ever-changing attack features (Han et al. 2017). This module can be extended to other industries where high real-time performance and service quality are desired (Wu and Hsu 2018).

The second stage of the framework quantifies losses for each kind of DDoS attack. We calculate quarterly losses for each DDoS type in the MMOG industry. The severity of the attacks also depends on their probability of occurrence. Thus, expected losses for each DDoS type provide a better estimation of the financial impact of these attacks (Mukhopadhyay et al. 2019). The expected loss distribution follows gamma distribution as they are positively skewed and long-tailed (Dutta and Perry 2011).

The third stage of the framework suggests ways to mitigate cyber-risk. CTOs of the MMOG firms have a crucial task in choosing mitigation strategies that do not bleed into profits and assures appropriate risk hedging when under cyber-attacks. In this study, we suggest four risk classes under which we have mapped different DDoS attack records. Attacks under high risk and high severity scenarios have to reduce their cyber-risk by subscribing to self-protection (Böhme and Kataria 2006; Johansmeyer 2021; Mukhopadhyay et al. 2019). Self-protection entails developing systems such as firewalls, backup CDNs, and intrusion detection systems. Attacks falling in high risk-low severity or low risk-high severity have a choice between self-insurance and cyber-insurance. They have to choose between the two substitutes depending upon the availability of budget, and in comparison, they will have to pay otherwise to the risk premium. Low risk-low severity attacks can straightaway subscribe to cyber-insurance because risk premiums are within acceptable limits for the range of risk values they bore. The extreme risk class (Hi-Hi) has to treat self-protection and cyber-insurance as compliments (Kesan et al. 2013; Majuca et al. 2006; Rejda 2007). The practice of subscribing to SI or CI disciplines the internal working of product development teams. It coerces them to be mindful of cybersecurity flaws and vulnerabilities that might otherwise make it susceptible to attacks (Austin and Darby 2003).

We contribute to the academic discussion by suggesting a novel variable and framework for cyber-risk management in the MMOG industry. Our study is one of the first studies to quantify and mitigate cyber-risk in MMO games using feedforward neural networks. The proposed model uses both attack-specific and MMOG platform-specific traits in quantifying cyber-risk. We also introduce novel variables incorporating a decreasing trend in vulnerabilities due to cybersecurity spending for quantifying cyber-risk. Lastly, we suggest cyber-insurance coupled with self-protection as a viable method to mitigate cyber-risk in the MMOG industry due to DDoS attacks.

MMOG firms value latency, scalability, and brand reputation as drivers of revenue. Our study has the following managerial implications. First, it provides CTOs with a tool with easy-to-understand steps and actionable insights in the form of cyber-risk management to mitigate DDoS attacks in the MMOG industry. The 2×2 cyber-risk mitigation heat-matrix provides exact mitigation steps along with probable investment strategies. Thus, managers could gauge whether the firm needs to invest in technology, cyber-insurance, or both. These mitigation strategies will discourage the hackers from causing financial loss to the firm and increase customer confidence in the authenticity of MMOG firms' offerings.

The current study is limited by the use of a proxy for cybersecurity spending. The MMOG firms strategically guard the actual data about the cybersecurity budget, and thus, its availability would improve the model's accuracy. We have used anonymized cyber attack data; therefore, firm-level variables do not form part of the model. Better datasets with firm-level details will improve the accuracy and validity of the model further. Using alternate data sources such as hacker forums and online gaming community discussions can help predict imminent DDoS attacks by incorporating a sliver of hacker behavior.

7.1.4. Text mining-based cyber-risk assessment for DDoS attacks and mitigation using cyber-insurance (TCRAM)

The first stage of the framework deals with the cyber-risk assessment, which concurs with prior studies to identify risky assets in a cyber-enabled firm (Bandyopadhyay and Mookerjee, 2019; Biswas and Mukhopadhyay, 2018; Das *et al.*, 2019; Gordon *et al.*, 2003; Mukhopadhyay *et al.*, 2019; Sharma and Mukhopadhyay, 2020a). We have used LDA-based topic modeling (Blei *et al.*, 2003) to extract themes related to different modules of cyber-risk management of DDoS attacks. We observe three central themes that emerge from both bigram and trigram bag-of-words models. These themes concern probable attack mechanisms, the cost of these attacks, and the firm's response strategy. A Kernel Naïve Bayes classifier follows it to predict the probability of correctly detecting traits of DDoS attacks from text articles (Mukhopadhyay *et al.*, 2019; Sharma and Mukhopadhyay, 2020a). Our model correctly identifies themes related to cyber-risk assessment (such as attack mechanism, top management response), which concurs with extant literature (Biswas *et al.*, 2021; Campbell *et al.*, 2003; Mukhopadhyay *et al.*, 2017; Tripathi and Mukhopadhyay, 2020). It also correctly identifies topics on cyber-risk mitigation (such as customer trust management, analytics-based intelligent response), which agrees with previous studies (Benaroch, 2002). In line with previous studies, topics related to Cyber-risk Quantification such as attack size, duration, and recovery cost are mostly misclassified (Angst *et al.*, 2012; Das *et al.*, 2019; Mukhopadhyay *et al.*, 2019). Attack traits are difficult to quantify immediately after the DDoS attacks due to the absence of any credible forensic data related to the attack mechanism or extent of the damage (Moody et al., 2017; Roy et al., 2015). The aforesaid framework quantifies the risk resulting from delayed or weak mitigation strategies due to misinterpretation of critical themes from web articles (Angst et al., 2012; Tripathi and Mukhopadhyay, 2020). Thus, the idea of threat appraisal of PMT is also validated through this module by estimation of likelihood of risk encountered due to misinterpretation of critical themes regarding DDoS attacks (Herath and Rao, 2009; Rogers, 1975).

DDoS attacks are primarily aimed at disrupting access to web servers, and thus, the duration of the attacks increases its severity (D'Arcy et al., 2020; Yue et al., 2019). The second stage of the framework quantifies losses for each misinterpretation of themes related to DDoS attacks. Our study uses expected loss as a proxy for the severity of DDoS attacks (Courtney, 1977; Mukhopadhyay et al., 2019). This module aims at quantifying the losses resulting from misinterpreting topics related to DDoS attacks. We observe that topics related to attack features such as intensity duration and revenue loss are the most misclassified and thus, result in larger expected losses (Angst et al., 2012; D'Arcy et al., 2020). We observe that such a delay results in losses as high as USD 2 million (Sharma and Mukhopadhyay, 2020c). These results are consistent with severity of fear appeals due to DDoS attacks in the threat appraisal component of protection-motivation theory (Herath and Rao, 2009; Rogers, 1975).

The third stage of the framework suggests ways to mitigate cyber-risk. CTOs of firms have a crucial task in choosing mitigation strategies that do not bleed into profits and assures appropriate risk hedging when under cyber-attacks (Benaroch, 2002; Biswas et al., 2021; Mukhopadhyay et al., 2019). In this study, we suggest four risk classes under which we have mapped different DDoS attack records. Attacks under high risk and high severity scenarios have to reduce their cyber-risk by subscribing to self-protection (Böhme and Kataria, 2006).

Self-protection entails developing firewalls, backup CDNs, intrusion detection systems (Böhme and Kataria, 2006; Herath and Herath, 2007). Prior studies have shown that it is easier to discourage hackers by strengthening the firm's cyber-defenses rather than deciphering different ways hackers attack cyber-systems (Chatterjee et al., 2015). Attacks falling in high risk-low severity or low risk-high severity have a choice between self-insurance and cyber-insurance. They have to choose between the substitutes depending upon the availability of budget, and in comparison, they would have paid as risk premium (Mukhopadhyay et al., 2019). Low risk-low severity attacks can straightaway subscribe to cyber-insurance because risk premiums are within acceptable limits. The extreme risk class (Hi-Hi) has to treat self-protection and cyber-insurance as compliments (Kesan et al., 2013; Majuca et al., 2006; Rejda, 2007). The practice of subscribing to Self-insurance or cyber-insurance disciplines the internal working of product development teams. It coerces them to be mindful of cybersecurity flaws and vulnerabilities that might otherwise make it susceptible to attacks (Austin and Darby, 2003). Consequently, we also position this module within the coping appraisal elucidated by protection-motivation theory. Our findings reaffirm the self-efficacy, response efficacy, and response cost components while choosing the optimal strategies amongst the numerous ways we could reduce risk as well as the severity of DDoS attacks (Herath and Rao, 2009; Rogers, 1975).

We contribute to the academic discussion by suggesting a framework to quantify the cyber-risk resulting from misinterpreting themes related to DDoS attacks from web articles, in line with threat and coping appraisal components of PMT. We suggest using a hybrid algorithm where a topic modeling technique such as LDA extracts themes from unstructured data such as web article text, followed by kernel Naïve Bayes classifier. THE KNB classifier aids in predicting the topic from bigrams (or trigrams). Our study contributes in the following ways.

Based on risk theory, we treat cyber-risk management as a tool to reduce risk and the severity of DDoS attacks to delayed mitigation by using cyber-risk management principles. Lastly, we suggest cyber-insurance coupled with self-protection as a viable method to mitigate cyber-risk due to DDoS attacks.

Firms value latency, scalability, and brand reputation as revenue drivers (D'Arcy *et al.*, 2020). Our study has the following managerial implications. First, it helps the CTOs summarize and analyze the unstructured data such as text from web articles and highlight areas of concern and actionable insights to counter their effects. Next, it provides CTOs with a tool with easy-to-understand steps and actionable insights in the form of cyber-risk management to mitigate DDoS. The 2×2 cyber-risk mitigation heat-matrix provides exact mitigation steps along with probable investment strategies. Thus, managers could gauge whether the firm needs to invest in technology, cyber-insurance, or both. It also helps the CTO stay proactive and well-versed with the latest developments around new cyberattacks and aids them in devising robust mitigation. These mitigation strategies will discourage the hackers' purpose of causing financial loss to the firm and increase customer's confidence in the authenticity of firms' offerings.

The current study is limited by its use of a proxy for cybersecurity spending. The firms strategically guard the actual data about the cybersecurity budget, and thus, its availability would improve the model's prediction quality. Firm-level variables do not form part of the model. Better datasets with firm-level details will improve the predictability and validity of the model further. Using alternate data sources such as hacker forums discussions can help predict imminent DDoS attacks by incorporating a sliver of hacker behavior.

7.2. Smart Cities

We undertake two studies in the context of cyber-risk management frameworks for smart cities.

7.2.1. SARIMA-based cyber-risk assessment and mitigation model for a smart city's traffic management systems (SCRAM)

This study investigates three main research questions, which also form the outline for the modules discussed henceforth. We try to devise a framework that addresses issues arising from road traffic disruption due to tampering of electronic speed limit signs in smart cities by hackers (Chatterjee et al. 2019; Pandey 2019). These attacks adversely impact commuters' productive time and smart cities' functioning as a whole.

The SCRAM model consists of three stages. The first stage (CRA) of the framework presented in our study addresses cyber risk assessment, following previous studies in which risky assets were identified in cyber-enabled firms (Biswas and Mukhopadhyay 2018; Courtney 1977; Gordon et al. 2003; Mukhopadhyay et al. 2019; Sharma and Mukhopadhyay 2020b). We used a SARIMA time-series forecasting model to predict (Geurts et al. 1977; Gujarati 2009; Kunreuther 1997b) the probability of ITMS sensors being tampered with, thus displaying an anomalous speed on the roads. We use the anomaly detection method to tag the anomalous average speeds and predict the proportion of such distortion due to cyberattacks. We observed that our CRA module performed well in estimating probability values for such misreads. This module identifies operational issues with integrated traffic systems in the smart city. It overcomes them to design a robust system with less congestion and reduced traffic fatalities, thus concurring with resilience theory (Hiller and Blanke 2017; Kitchin and Dodge 2019). Our model computes the probability of a hacker manipulating the ITMS speed limit sign and causing a misreading of the speed limit, aligning with the threat appraisal component/construct of the PMT (Herath and Rao 2009; Rogers 1975).

The second stage (CRQ) of the framework quantified the expected losses (i.e., severity) for each of the months following hacker-induced malfunctioning of ITMS sensors (Sharma and

Mukhopadhyay 2021b; Wu et al. n.d.; Xu et al. 2019). Our model's severity computation for anomalous speeds, which may result in congestion/collision, is in line with the threat appraisal component of the PMT (Herath and Rao 2009; Rogers 1975).

Based on rational choice theory (Becker 1978; McCarthy 2002), the CRM module suggests various strategies to mitigate cyber risks estimated in the second stage (CRQ) of the framework to quantify the expected losses (i.e., severity) for each of the month's speed anomalies (Puiu et al. 2016). Smart-city administrators have the crucial task of choosing mitigation strategies that are not cost-prohibitive and ensuring appropriate risk hedging during cyberattacks. In this study, we suggest four risk classes under which we mapped different speed misreading scenarios. Administrators should reduce the probability of speed misreadings in the high-risk and high-severity quadrant by strengthening the smart city's cyber-defenses, such as firewalls, backup CDNs, and intrusion detection systems (Cavusoglu et al. 2005, 2009; Kenyon et al. n.d.; Mukhopadhyay et al. 2019). Smart cities experiencing cyberattacks in the high-risk and low-severity quadrant (or low-risk and high-severity) may choose between self-insurance and cyber-insurance depending on budget availability (Bojanc and Jerman-Blažič 2008; Hartwig and Wilkinson 2014). Smart cities facing cyberattacks in the low-risk and low-severity quadrant can subscribe to cyber-insurance because their risk premiums are within acceptable limits. It forces smart cities to be more mindful of cybersecurity vulnerabilities and their mitigation (He and Zhang 2019; Lee et al. 2020). CRM strategies follow from the coping appraisal component of the PMT, where we evaluate the response efficacy along with self-efficacy and response cost (Herath and Rao 2009; Rogers 1975).

This study identifies a smart-city ecosystem's key stakeholders: citizens, smart-city administration, and hackers (Ullah et al. 2021). Next, we model the workflow of ITMS and ways in which hackers can compromise it. We propose a SARIMA based model to forecast the average speed of vehicles as recorded by the ITMS sensors. Second, we devise scenarios in which these sensors can be compromised across each month. We use the anomaly prediction module to tag day hours with anomalous speeds from hacker-induced manipulation (Puiu et al. 2016). We observed that our CRA module performed well in estimating probability values for such misreads. The final output from the CRA module computes the probability of detecting these speed anomalies and subsequently the expected loss caused by each. Our CRM module, based on general detection theory, proposes the use of perimeter security to deter hackers from resorting to speed limit disruption. Additionally, we propose using financial mitigation strategies such as cyber-insurance policies to reduce the impact of such anomalies on the smart-city ecosystem (Cheng et al. 2020; Elmaghraby and Losavio 2014; Xu et al. 2019).

This study uses empirical evidence from ITMA sensors to estimate cyber risks and their associated losses. Limited quantitative studies on software-defined networks (SDNs) in smart cities have explored similar premises (Chen et al. 2020). They used a cyber-attack vector in SDNs to estimate losses. Our methodology uses unique speed sensor data and reveals a potential mediating channel between cyber risks and sensor obfuscation in smart cities. Qualitative studies elucidating frameworks to assess smart city success have been suggested in the past (Dhillon and Backhouse 2000; Dhillon and Torkzadeh 2006). Our approach builds upon it and tries to quantify the cyber risk accrued through different levels of interoperability. We also contribute by employing time-series forecasting methods to estimate cyber-risk and suggest ways to mitigate them in smart cities.

Our model provides the city administrators with a heat matrix (i.e., of risk × severity) (Mukhopadhyay et al. 2019), which details the different risky scenarios arising from hacker-induced speed manipulation through ITMS sensors. The city administrator can prioritize risk mitigation strategies (Böhme and Kataria 2006; Kesan et al. 2013; Majuca et al. 2006; Rejda

2007). First, they need to address the risk in the high risk-high severity quadrant by resorting to self-protection measures such as perimeter security as a deterrence (Guarro 1987) and predictive technological intervention (Zhang et al. 2021). As a result, the risk shifts to the low risk-high severity quadrant. The administrator can then self-insure to move such scenarios to the low risk-low severity quadrant (Choo et al. 2021). Subsequently, city administrators can pass the residual risk onto a third-party cyber insurer (Böhme and Schwartz 2006; Kesan et al. 2005; Rejda 2007).

7.2.2. Cyber-risk Assessment and Mitigation framework for smart cities: A deep learning approach (DL-CRAM)

This study investigates three main research questions, which also form the outline for the modules discussed henceforth. We try to devise a framework that addresses issues arising from road traffic disruption due to tampering of electronic speed limit signs in smart cities by hackers (Bandyopadhyay and Mookerjee 2019; Kitchin and Dodge 2019). The first stage (CRA) of the framework presented in our study addresses cyber risk assessment, following previous studies in which risky assets were identified in cyber-enabled firms (Biswas and Mukhopadhyay 2018; Courtney 1977; Gordon et al. 2003; Han et al. 2017; Mukhopadhyay et al. 2019; Sharma and Mukhopadhyay 2020c). We used a CNN model to classify (Kunreuther 1997b; LeCun et al. 1989) to predict the probability for each scenario of misreading the speed limit signs on the roads. We use Bayesian inference to calculate the probability of three risky scenarios when only the first, second, or both digits are misread (Hastie et al. 2009; I. B. Hossack et al. 1999). Our CRA module performed well in estimating probability values, which aligns with the threat appraisal component of PMT and resilience theory (Awad et al. 2019; Herath and Rao 2009; Hiller and Blanke 2017; Rogers 1975).

The second stage (CRQ) of the framework quantified the expected losses (i.e., severity) for each of the misreading scenarios when only the first, second, or both digits are misread (Alsop 2021; Becker 1978; Han et al. 2017; Mukhopadhyay et al. 2019). The severity computation also aligns with the threat appraisal component of the PMT (Herath and Rao 2009; Rogers 1975) and risk theory (Kunreuther 1997b).

Based on rational choice theory (Becker 1978), the CRM module suggests various strategies to mitigate cyber-risk for each scenario where only the first, second, or both digits are misread (Benaroch 2002). If only the first digit is wrongly read in this study, we suggest reducing the risk before passing it on to a third-party cyber-insurer (Austin and Darby 2003; Herath and Herath 2007; Mukhopadhyay et al. 2019; Rejda 2007). Similarly, if a second digit or both are misread, they can directly pass it on to a cyber-insurer. CRM strategies align with the coping appraisal component of the PMT (Herath and Rao 2009; Rogers 1975).

This study identifies the key stakeholders of a smart-city ecosystem (Israilidis et al. 2019) and models the workflows of ITMS and how hackers can disrupt them. First, we propose a deep learning-based approach for a smart city (Herath and Rao 2009; Lee et al. 2004). It is in line with the threat and coping appraisal components of PMT. Second, we devise three risky scenarios along with risk and severity calculations. We use the Bayesian inference method (Hastie et al. 2009) to infer three risky scenarios emanating from hacker-induced manipulation (Awad et al. 2019). We observed that our CRA module performed well in estimating probability values for such misreads. The final output from the CRA module computes the probability of detecting these speed limit misreadings and, subsequently, the expected loss caused by each. Our CRM module proposes perimeter security to deter hackers from resorting to speed limit disruption, as mentioned in the above risky scenarios (Lee et al. 2004). Additionally, we propose using financial mitigation strategies such as cyber-insurance policies

(Kesan et al. 2013; Rejda 2007) to reduce the impact of such anomalies on the smart-city ecosystem (Manfreda et al. 2021).

Our model provides the city administrators with a heat matrix (i.e., of risk × severity) (Westerman and Hunter 2007), which details the different risky scenarios arising from hacker-induced speed limit sign manipulation. The city administrator can prioritize risk mitigation strategies (Böhme and Schwartz 2006, 2010; Kesan et al. 2013). As a result, the risk reduces; thereby, the administrator can self-insure (Rejda 2007). Subsequently, city administrators can pass the residual risk onto a third-party cyber insurer (Chatterjee et al. 2015; Kesan et al. 2005; Rejda 2007).

7.3. Crowdfunding platforms

Crowdfunding platforms have been plagued with issues of campaign authenticity of campaigns. Many creators have launched fake campaigns to fraud the masses. Thus, it becomes crucial for these platforms to ensure an automated method to identify successful campaigns or otherwise. Our model consists of three stages (or modules). The first stage of the framework deals with the cyber-risk assessment, which concurs with prior studies to identify risky assets in a cyber-enabled firm (Bandyopadhyay and Mookerjee 2019; Biswas and Mukhopadhyay 2018; Das et al. 2019; Gordon et al. 2003; Mukhopadhyay et al. 2019; Sharma and Mukhopadhyay 2020). We have used the Kernel naïve Bayes classifier to predict the probability of success and failure of campaigns. We concur with earlier studies that highlighted the traits of successful campaigns (Gordon et al. 2003; O'Reilly et al. 2018).

The second stage of the framework quantifies losses for the crowdfunding platform for misclassification of success or failure of a campaign. Our study uses expected loss as a proxy for the severity of loss platform fees (Courtney 1977; Mukhopadhyay et al. 2019). The third stage of the framework suggests ways to mitigate cyber-risk. CTOs of the crowdfunding platforms have a crucial task in choosing mitigation strategies that do not bleed into profits and assure appropriate risk hedging when campaigns that fail increase. This study suggests four risk classes under which we have mapped different campaigns and success states. Campaigns under high-risk and high-severity scenarios have to reduce their cyber-risk by subscribing to self-protection (Böhme and Kataria 2006). Self-protection entails developing technology-based solutions entailing consortium blockchain solutions (Böhme and Kataria 2006; Herath and Herath 2007). Low risk-low severity attacks can straightaway onboard the platform. The extreme risk class (Hi-Hi) has to treat self-protection and blockchain-based solution as compliments (Kesan et al. 2013; Majuca et al. 2006; Rejda 2007).

We contribute by suggesting a novel method of reducing the number of fraud campaigns by improving the campaign data quality and thereby, boosting the accuracy with which the Kernel naïve Bayes classifier identifies the successful campigns. Crowdfunding platforms value the onboarding of successful campaigns and reducing failed campaigns. Our study provides CTOs with a tool with easy-to-understand steps and actionable insights in the form of cyber-risk management to handle misclassification of campaigns as successful or failure.

8. Conclusion

This thesis provides decision-makers (such as CTOs and smart city administrators) tools to mitigate cyber-risk arising through cyber-attacks and value disruptions in the digital ecosystems such as MMOG platforms, smart cities, and crowdfunding platforms. Firstly, we propose four studies pertaining to MMOG platforms. We follow a process-view approach to design studies emulating how MMOG firms respond to cyberattacks in a phased manner due to an absence of credible vulnerability data at the first instance of attack. We proceed across models in alignment with the way firms augment attack data with vulnerability and cybersecurity spending data. Our studies for MMOG firms provide CTOs with a tool to ensure the pursuit of performance, which is critical in MMO games. We estimated the probability of different DDoS attacks occurring in the MMOG industry. We used a kernel naïve Bayes classifier, generalized linear models, and artificial neural networks to predict the probability of each type of DDoS attack. Next, we used risk analysis principles and calculated the expected loss values. In the last stage of the study, we analyzed the risk (i.e., probability of the attack) and severity (i.e., expected loss of attacks) of different types of attacks to suggest ways to mitigate cyber-risk. Our frameworks help MMOG firms face high-risk/high-severity attacks by offering cyber-insurance and self-protection strategies. We also propose a text mining-based framework to monitor web articles related to cyberattacks proactively and quantify the cyber-risk emanating due to misclassification of critical themes leading to incorrect or delayed mitigation. We posit that a CTO performs threat appraisal of their firms' potential vulnerabilities and estimates the monetary impact on their business, in line with the PMT. This study analyzes the web articles related to DDoS attacks to summarize their causes, quantifies their monetary impact on business, and devises mitigation strategies. The hybrid topic clustering and classification model uses a KNB classifier and LDA-based topic modeling approach to calculate the probability of detecting a topic in the DDoS attack-related text corpus and the expected losses and suggest subsequent mitigation strategies. In 90 percent of cases, the classifier could detect the topic correctly from the text corpus. Based on risk theory, we also aid the CTO in deciding whether to accept, reduce, or transfer the cyber-risk using technological interventions and cyber-insurance.

We also propose two studies related to cyber-risk issues in smart cities. We observed that hackers compromise Integrated Traffic Management Systems (ITMS) in smart cities by using two probable paths. They tamper with electronic speed limit signs, spoofing in-vehicle sensors to misread speed and result in congestion or collision situations. Secondly, we posit that hackers can also tamper with ITMS speed sensors at street intersections to cause traffic congestion or overspeeding problems on smart city pathways. Across the studies, we first model the threat appraisal for a smart-city administrator regarding the probability of a hacker distorting benign components such as ITMS speed sensors and electronic speed limit signs, resulting in a vehicle collision or congestion situation. We use time series-based and deep learning methods to estimate the probability of sensors generating incorrect average speed data, respectively. Next, we calculate the threat appraisal for smart-city administrators regarding the severity of monetary losses resulting from congestion and collision in smart-city pathways from hacker-induced distortions. Subsequently, we suggest cyber risk mitigation strategies for smart-city administrators according to coping appraisal mechanisms, including technological deterrents (such as perimeter security) and financial tools such as cyber-insurance policies.

Lastly, we identified traits necessary for the success of campaigns on crowdfunding platforms and suggested ways for their improvement using blockchain-based crowdfunding models. We found out that both external and platform-specific traits of a creator play an essential role in deciding the success of a campaign. On the other hand, a lower goal amount, low backer ratio, and shorter duration of campaign run ensure the success of a campaign. We estimate the probability of different campaigns succeeding. We use a Kernel Naïve Bayes classifier to predict the probability of success of campaigns. Next, we use risk analysis principles and calculate the expected loss values. The last stage of the study uses risk (i.e., probability of the attack) and severity (i.e., expected loss of attacks) to suggest ways to mitigate cyber-risk. Our model helps platforms with high-risk and high-severity campaigns by offering a consortium-based blockchain solution to eliminate fraudulent campaigns and improve the campaign data quality for algorithm-based onboarding of campaigns in the future. Thus, this thesis suggests how decision-makers prioritize cyber-risk by either reducing, accepting, or passing it using an optimal mix of technological and financial interventions such as cyber-insurance.

Printed in the USA
CPSIA information can be obtained
at www.ICGtesting.com
LVHW021342051023
760085LV00064B/1852